INDIGENOUS POLITICAL
OF WESTERN MAL___

91

LONDON SCHOOL OF ECONOMICS
MONOGRAPHS ON SOCIAL ANTHROPOLOGY

Managing Editor: Anthony Forge

The Monographs on Social Anthropology were established in 1940 and aim to publish results of modern anthropological research of primary interest to specialists.

The continuation of the series was made possible by a grant in aid from the Wenner-Gren Foundation for Anthropological Research, and more recently by a further grant from the Governors of the London School of Economics and Political Science.

The Monographs are under the direction of an Editorial Board associated with the Department of Anthropology of the London School of Economics and Political Science.

LONDON SCHOOL OF ECONOMICS
MONOGRAPHS ON SOCIAL ANTHROPOLOGY
No. 17

Indigenous
Political Systems of
Western Malaya

by

J. M. GULLICK

UNIVERSITY OF LONDON
THE ATHLONE PRESS
NEW YORK: HUMANITIES PRESS INC.

First published in 1958 *by*
THE ATHLONE PRESS
UNIVERSITY OF LONDON
at 2 *Gower Street, London,* WC1

Distributed by Constable & Co Ltd
12 *Orange Street, London,* WC2

Canada
Oxford University Press
Toronto

Reprinted 1965

Library of Congress Catalog Card No. 65–16340

First printed in 1958 *by*
J. W. ARROWSMITH LTD
BRISTOL

Reprinted in 1965 *by photo-litho by*
WILLIAM CLOWES AND SONS LTD
BECCLES

Preface

This study was submitted and accepted as a thesis for the Academic Postgraduate Diploma in Anthropology of the University of London. Some minor alterations, mainly of internal arrangement, have been made in preparing it for publication.

The use of the term 'lineage' is dictated by lack of a suitable alternative. Malay aristocrats were more conscious of their individual status by descent than of group loyalties based on common descent. But, as is explained in Chapter 4, they were on occasion united in group solidarity against others when the political office which was the basis of their status was in jeopardy (see pp. 70–2).

I should like to express my gratitude to Professor Raymond Firth and to Dr. Maurice Freedman for their help and encouragement during the eight years of my intermittent studies for the Diploma.

J.M.G.

London
December 1956

Contents

I

Introduction

The purpose of this study is to describe and analyse the political institutions of the western Malay States as they were in the period just before coming under British control in 1874. The 'western Malay States' are for this purpose Perak, Selangor and Negri Sembilan. Some additional data have also been taken from Pahang and Kedah.

So far as the use of purely documentary sources permits, the aim has been to present indigenous Malay political institutions of the period as a working system of social control and leadership in the same fashion as an anthropologist uses material obtained by contemporary fieldwork. This method has been used before, notably in Professor Firth's *Primitive Economics of the New Zealand Maori*, but so far as I am aware no study on these lines has been made before in the field of Malay studies.

There is of course a substantial literature on nineteenth-century Malaya. The Appendix[1] on sources acknowledges my reliance on the writings, especially the unpublished administrative records, of the first generation of British administrators in the Malay States after 1874. Much has also been written since by scholars (some of them also administrators). The contributions of R. J. Wilkinson and Sir Richard Winstedt in almost every field of Malay studies are so outstanding as to require no comment here. More recently modern historical research, especially by Dr. C. D. Cowan has added much to our knowledge of the course of events in the third quarter of the nineteenth century.

Previous writers have been mainly concerned with one or other of two themes. As a matter of straightforward history, political conditions in the Malay States in the years before 1874 contributed to the British decision to intervene and take control. In accounts of these matters the focus of interest has been upon the disorder and on the weakness of the Sultans as rulers. This situation tends to be compared with the reforms and the economic progress of the period after 1874.

By contrast writers on Malay political institutions have rejected the 1870 period as an era of degeneration and have essayed to describe Malay institutions as they were believed to have been in their prime. The result is not history but a reflection of late nineteenth-century Malay tradition of what their political system was supposed to have been long ago. It is

[1]See p. 144

an ideal pattern rather than an account of a situation which ever existed.

These two viewpoints taken together present a Golden Age, which like all social myths is timeless, followed by a Dark Age (c.1870) which is an interval between the passing of the heroes and the coming of the proconsuls.

This study is concerned with the situation of 1870 as a working social system adapted to the needs of its community. Various factors described hereafter[1] led to a decentralized system of local government by district

[1] See pp. 17, 127, and 133.

chiefs. The Sultans exercised little real power. But the Sultanate and the ancient institutional forms of the State Government played their part in systems of symbolism and status. They were needed not as media for the exercise of power but as a 'charter' or justification for the political system

which gave power to others. The geographical environment and historical background are a necessary preface to further explanation of this hypothesis.

GEOGRAPHY

The main geographical feature of north and central Malaya is a series of ranges of hills 'which lie staggered *en echelon* and skew-wise across the peninsula on NNE–SSW lines'.[1] This central spine of hills forms the main watershed of the Malay Peninsula. Since the Malay States, the major political units, were centred on river valleys, the central watershed was

[1] Dobby (1950), p. 87.

also a political boundary. The western Malay States lie between the central ranges and the west coast.

The area of the three western states is:

STATE	AREA[1] (sq. miles)
Perak	7,980
Selangor	3,166
Negri Sembilan	2,550
Total	13,606

The State of Perak takes its name from the Perak River and it consists mainly of the basin of that river which rises at a point just south of latitude 6° north and runs south to enter the Straits of Malacca at about 4° north. The axis of the state is thus north to south. In addition to the Perak River basin the State of Perak also includes a narrow coastal strip separated from the western limit of the river basin by one of the lesser north–south ranges. This coastal strip is the Larut/Krian area. Selangor, between 3° 50' and 2° 30' north, takes its name from the Selangor River, but in 1870 it comprised the basins of five rivers which run in a general east–west direction from the central watershed to the Straits of Malacca. The five rivers of Selangor were (from north to south) the Bernam, the Selangor, the Klang, the Langat and the Lukut[2] rivers. Negri Sembilan between 3° 20' and 2° 20' north covers the basins of the Linggi River and the upper reaches of the Muar River.

Although mountains (rising at their highest to 6–7,000 feet) were the most notable natural feature, they were empty spaces in terms of human settlement; the ranges were lines of division not of concentration. It was the coastal flats, the river banks and, to a lesser extent, the undulating land between hills and sea which attracted and supported human settlement.

The main features[3] of the climate were, and are, (1) a uniformly high temperature throughout the year ranging between a daily minimum of 70°F and a daily maximum of 90°F without notable seasonal variation and (2) an extremely heavy rainfall spread over all months of the year. In most parts of the Malay Peninsula annual rainfall totals are between the limits 75–125 inches but in some places, including an area in Perak, annual rainfall is as much as 175 inches or more. The incidence of rainfall is somewhat affected by the monsoonal seasons with two peaks during the year in April/May and in October/November. There are however no dry seasons.

---

[1] These are the areas of the modern States. There have been some minor frontier modifications since 1870 but these have not significantly affected the areas of the states.

[2] Lukut is now part of Negri Sembilan.

[3] Dobby (1950), pp. 92–5.

The significant aspects of the climate are the lack of marked seasonal change and the abundance of water both for agriculture and for keeping the rivers full and navigable to boats throughout the year. The soil is generally poor and deteriorates rapidly, especially by water erosion on slopes, if the natural forest cover is removed. But in some valley and coastal areas there are very fertile alluvial soils accumulated by run-off from the higher ground of the interior owing to the erosive action of the rivers. The rivers because of their association with exceptionally fertile estuarial areas (among other reasons) were a most significant feature in the human geography of the 1870's.

At that time the natural cover of tropical rain forest had been little disturbed by a sparse population.[1] From the inland edge of the coastal fringe of mangrove swamps the jungle extended almost unbroken to the summits of the central ranges. The overhead foliage is sometimes dense enough to keep the ground beneath it clear of undergrowth but more typically there is a thicket of saplings, creepers and shrubs at ground level which makes the jungle impassable unless a path is laboriously hacked through it. In the 1870's, when there were no roads, everyone travelled by boat on the rivers if he could in preference to journeys overland. This factor also contributed to making the river lines very important.

The Malayan jungle is evergreen and if untouched persists unchanged for ever. But if the jungle is felled to clear land for cultivation and is later abandoned, a thick secondary forest appears (called *belukar* in Malay) consisting of young trees, ferns, grass and scrub. If however the soil has been badly eroded or impoverished before it is abandoned, it tends to become covered by an all-pervasive coarse, tall grass known as *lallang* (*imperata cylindrica*) rather than by secondary forest.

The last natural feature which requires mention is the alluvial deposits of tin. Tin ore (*cassiterite*) is found in gravels and sands, often buried some feet below an overburden of non-productive soil in various places (usually river valleys) of the low country. In the 1870's the main deposits being worked were at Larut and Kinta in Perak, at Kuala Lumpur in Selangor and around Seremban in Sungei Ujong (Negri Sembilan). The famous mining centre of Lukut had gone into a decline about 1870 as the deposits considered workable at that time were exhausted.

It is known that Larut at its peak before the outbreak of the miners' civil war in 1872 produced 800 *bahara* of tin per month.[2] This was an annual output of 1,700 tons worth £70,000 at the prices then prevailing. Output at Kuala Lumpur in the early 1870's was estimated at 1,000 *bahara* of tin per month,[3] i.e. about 2,000 tons p.a. worth about £80,000.

---

[1] Over Perak, Selangor and Negri Sembilan together population averaged less than 10 persons per square mile.

[2] *JMBRAS* (1953), xxvi, pt 3, p. 93. A *bahara* was 400 lb.

[3] Purcell (1948), p. 102.

Output at Kinta and Sungei Ujong was of the order of 1,000 tons of tin p.a. at each place.[1] In all mining areas however working population and output fluctuated sharply from year to year. In addition to the large and important mining centres there were innumerable other small mines up and down the country. But almost all the known tin deposits of the Malay Peninsula were in Perak, Selangor, Negri Sembilan and (to a lesser extent) in Pahang. Malay chiefs taxed tin mines in various ways and thus diverted into their own hands from a fifth to a third of the value of the output. Revenue from tin was the mainstay of the Malay political system.

Tin had been mined and exported from Malaya for centuries. Until about 1820 tin mining had been entirely in the hands of Malays. The Malay technique was to dig out the 'pay dirt' (known as *karang*) and to shovel it into a stream of running water. The heavy particles of ore fell to the bottom while the earth was carried away by the stream. The ore was then smelted in a charcoal furnace and cast into ingots. About 1820 the practice began of importing immigrant Chinese labour from the provinces of Kwangtung and Fukien in south China to work as tin miners in Malaya. These Chinese worked full-time at the mines in contrast to the Malays for whom mining was often an intermittent occupation. The Chinese were able to work down to a greater depth because they were there every day to bale out the flood-water which was the bane of open-cast mining. Moreover they adapted the chain-pump and the waterwheel to make mechanical pumps for dewatering their mines. It may be that this apparatus was part of the agricultural equipment of their homes in China. By sustained labour and primitive mechanization the Chinese were able to work down to deeper and richer deposits than Malays. Between 1840 and 1860 the major mining areas had passed into the occupation and use of Chinese miners under an accommodation with Malay chiefs to be described later.[2]

HISTORY

The history of the Malays formed a notable part of their culture. Their earliest written history (the *Sejarah Melayu*—'Malay Annals') was written about 1540[3] and they had a large and varied literature beginning from that period but recording the traditions of still earlier periods. Their literature was in the romantic style—the encounters of kings and magicians, the exploits of heroic fighting men and so on. There is a

---

[1] It was reckoned (*JMBRAS*, xxiv, pt 2, p. 90) that on the average a miner produced two *bahara* of tin (800 lb) in the course of a year. At both Kinta and Sungei Ujong the working population fluctuated but was generally above 3,000—especially at Sungei Ujong.

[2] See below, pp. 24 and 126.

[3] Winstedt, *JMBRAS* (1940), xvii, pt 3, p. 107. See also C. C. Brown's translation of the *Malay Annals* published as *JMBRAS* (1952), xxv, pts 2 and 3.

certain amount of historical fact embedded in it. But its main significance
in the context of social analysis is that Malay literature and history served
to transmit the traditions and values of the community, more especially
of its ruling class.

The Malays were not the first-comers to the Peninsula. Long before
their arrival there was a migration, apparently not on a large scale, of
negrito, proto-Malay and other hunting and collecting tribes who were
generally described by the Malays as *Sakai* and regarded as aborigines.
These primitive peoples withdrew into the hills and had little contact
with the later Malay immigrants. Malay chiefs in Negri Sembilan were
wont to derive their titles to land from putative descent from Sakai
ancestresses who were said to have intermarried with Malay immigrants.[1]
The contacts of the nineteenth century consisted mainly of a little trading
and some slave-raiding of Sakai by Malays.

The Malays are members of the Indonesian group of Mongoloid
peoples. It is generally accepted[2] that the Indonesians migrated south-
wards from south-west China (Yunnan) some 3,000 years ago. The first
areas of Malay settlement in the Peninsula were perhaps in the extreme
north and south (Kelantan, Kedah and Johore) rather than in the central
states with which this study is concerned. But traces of neolithic and
bronze age cultures have been found in many places.[3]

Up to about 1400 A.D. Malaya lay on the periphery of various political
units centred elsewhere in the Indonesian archipelago or even further
away. Early in the Christian era there were outposts in north Malaya of
Hindu kingdoms centred on Annam in Indo-China and the Coromandel
coast of India.[4] In the seventh century the Malay Peninsula fell within
the sphere of the Sumatran Buddhist kingdom of Sri Vijaya. In the
fourteenth century the Javanese kingdom of Majapahit overwhelmed Sri
Vijaya. About 1400 A.D. a Malay prince from Tumasik (the modern
Singapore) established a dynasty at Malacca on the west coast. This
event marked the beginning of an indigenous system of major political
units in the Malay Peninsula.

The Malacca Sultanate was the heroic period in the historical traditions
of the Peninsula Sultanates which succeeded it. It lasted only a century
(c. 1400–1511) but its influence was immense. The later Malay States
inherited from Malacca both a tradition in which some of their major
values were expressed and also a pattern or form of political organization
which it was their pride to preserve.

Certain aspects of the Malacca Sultanate are thus of considerable
significance.[5] The rulers of Malacca reproduced on a smaller scale the

[1] See, e.g., Gullick (1949), p. 8–9 for Sungei Ujong myths.
[2] Winstedt (1935), p. 14.
[3] See Tweedie (1953), and Linehan, *JMBRAS* (1951), xxiv, pt. 3, p. 1.
[4] Quaritch Wales (1940, 1947).
[5] This brief account is based on Winstedt (1935) and Wilkinson (1924).

political system of the earlier kingdoms of western Indonesia. The head
and centre of the system was a ruler drawn from a royal patrilineage,
his authority buttressed by some of the 'divine king' attributes of earlier
Hindu dynasties. Under the direction of the ruler and of other princes of
the royal house the business of government was carried on by ministers
or executives (*mentri*) from aristocratic but non-royal lineages. There was
a hierarchy of greater and lesser offices. Among the more important of
the officers of state were the *Bendahara* (Chief Minister), the *Temenggong*
(Commander of Troops and Police), the *Penghulu Bendahari* (Treasurer),
Mentri (Secretary of State) and the *Shahbandar* (Harbour Master and
Collector of Customs).

The relative importance of the *Shahbandar* is a clue to the nature of the
regime. Malacca and its rival States of the Straits of Malacca were essentially trade centres. For this purpose Malacca was well situated on the
sea route from India to China. In the early fifteenth century the Malacca
Sultans were sending trade missions to China. In the early sixteenth
century the Portuguese were aided in their attack on Malacca by the
defection of the Indian, Chinese and other foreign merchants of Malacca
resentful at the exactions of their Malay rulers. The Malacca Sultanate
was a compact and centralized political system which lived on the foreign
trade of its port.

There were of course outlying districts and political officers for the
administration of those districts. For example, one of the most famous of
the Bendaharas of Malacca had, earlier in his career, been district governor
of Klang at the mouth of the Klang River, a tin-producing area, while
the foundation of the royal dynasty of Perak was ascribed to an elder
son of a Sultan of Malacca sent into remote obscurity in Perak in order
to leave the field clear for the succession to the throne of Malacca of a
favourite younger son. These instances serve to show that the seat of
power was at the centre—in Malacca. The royal dynasty and the great
officers of state were all gathered there. The administration of outlying
trade posts was of minor importance.

In 1511 the Portuguese captured Malacca and made it a strongpoint of
their maritime empire. In 1641 the Dutch captured Malacca from the
Portuguese and succeeded to their position as the dominant European
power in the Straits of Malacca. The emphasis of Dutch administration
was on the promotion of trade with the Malay States. In 1795 the British
took Malacca. As a result of the settlement following the end of the
Napoleonic War the British gained recognition of an exclusive sphere of
influence among the central and southern states of the Malay Peninsula
(the northern states were tributaries of Siam). The British position in
Malaya in the mid-nineteenth century was based on the three Straits
Settlements of Penang, Malacca and Singapore administered by a governor
resident at Singapore. The Straits Settlements became highly successful
centres of trade with neighbouring areas of the Malay Peninsula and of

Indonesia. Large mercantile communities, European, Chinese and Indian, grew up in British ports. It was they, especially the Chinese, who organized the development of Chinese tin-mining in the Malay States. It thus became inevitable that there should eventually be direct action by the British authorities in the Straits Settlements to protect the investments of their merchants in the Malay States. But, until late 1873, the British policy was to promote trade in the Malay States, to prevent the outbreak of war between States, but to abstain from anything more active than occasional missions of mediation to the Malay States.

The Malay Sultans of Malacca and their nobles after being expelled from Malacca by the Portuguese in 1511 eventually established themselves in Johore at the extreme southern end of the Malay Peninsula. From this base they fought desultory wars with the Portuguese and with their rivals among the trade states of the Straits of Malacca. Pahang became a sort of detached province under an independent ruler of non-royal descent who owed only formal allegiance to Johore. The Sultans of Perak, established in the State before the fall of Malacca, persisted as a weak but independent dynasty. At the start of the eighteenth century Bugis adventurers from the Celebes obtained control of the Johore Sultanate as 'underkings' (*Yam Tuan Muda*) to the impotent Sultans. A branch of this Bugis dynasty established itself at Klang and at the mouth of the Selangor River; this area was historically a dependency of the Malacca Sultanate. During the eighteenth century the Bugis rulers of Selangor obtained general recognition as a royal dynasty but only after much bitter fighting with Sumatran kingdoms.

Negri Sembilan[1] had developed on rather different lines. It had been a dependency of the Sultans of Malacca in the fifteenth century and they had appointed district headmen. After the fall of the Malacca Sultanate these headmen persisted and maintained formal relations with the Sultans of Johore. There was no focus of central government in Negri Sembilan itself at this time. In the sixteenth century and after there was a substantial immigration into Negri Sembilan of settlers from Menangkabau in Sumatra. The long-established ruling families became culturally assimilated to the matrilineal social system of the later arrivals from Menangkabau. Negri Sembilan thus became a loose aggregate of independent minor states (the name 'Negri Sembilan' means 'Nine States') ruled by chiefs whose lineages, like those of their immigrant subjects, were based on matrilineal descent. During the eighteenth century the Negri Sembilan confederacy became involved in wars with the Bugis warriors from Johore and Selangor. In order to have a single military defence commander in these wars the four principal district chiefs of Negri Sembilan (the *Undang* of the districts of Sungei Ujong, Rembau, Jelebu and Johol) invited over a prince from the royal family of Menangkabau to be their overlord (*Yang-di-pertuan Besar*) but with very limited powers. This was the

---

[1] Information from Wilkinson (1911). See also Gullick (1949).

B

origin of the office of royal ruler of Negri Sembilan. At first however it was not an hereditary office. The first three rulers were invited over from Menangkabau to hold office for life only. According to the tradition each married the daughter of his predecessor. At all events a royal dynasty gradually emerged and by the first quarter of the nineteenth century it was established, not without fighting, that the royal office was to descend within the royal patrilineage, generally to a son or brother of the previous ruler.

The political system of Perak, Selangor and Negri Sembilan was related to a common model despite considerable differences of detail. Perak may be regarded as conforming closely to the traditional norm. Its royal dynasty was (or claimed to be) descended from the Sultans of Malacca. The non-royal offices of state were organized on the standard basis of four chiefs of the first rank, eight of the second and sixteen of the third. Negri Sembilan and Selangor resembled Perak in constituting a state (Negri) as a major political unit with a royal ruler and a hierarchy of lesser office holders. Selangor however had a much smaller population than Perak[1] and for this reason could not support a large non-royal aristocracy in addition to the royal lineage. In Selangor therefore all offices of state were held by princes of the royal house. The royal house of Selangor contrasted with that of Perak in being of Bugis origin; it was thus invested with the aura of hostility and dislike which the Sumatran Malays had felt towards their Bugis enemies in the eighteenth century wars. This factor was important because a large part of the immigrant population in Selangor were of Sumatran origin. In general the Selangor ruling class had much less influence over their subjects than their opposite numbers in Perak. Negri Sembilan was different again. The powers of its ruling house were limited by a comparatively recent compact between the founder of the dynasty and the chiefs. In Negri Sembilan moreover the political system, except in the case of the royal dynasty, was based on matrilineal descent groups—a feature which did not appear in the other States.

Despite these contrasts Perak, Selangor and Negri Sembilan had more in common with each other than any of them had with other Malay States. Johore and Pahang lacked an acknowledged royal ruler (and all that went with such an office) until late in the nineteenth century. The Malay States to the north were nominal dependencies of Siam and their political system was affected by that fact. Perak, Selangor and Negri Sembilan were the main centres of Chinese tin-mining. They have been chosen as the subject of this study partly because of the accident that more information is available concerning their situation than of other States. But they are also instructive examples as a group in their similarities and in their differences.

The nineteenth century saw rapid changes in the political situation of these three States. Negri Sembilan, which had gathered a substantial

[1] See below, p. 23.

immigrant Malaysian population earlier than the other two states, already illustrated one trend. In all States the immigrant population spread over a number of localities and earned its living by mining and agriculture—in contrast to the 'trade centre' pattern of settlement of the Malacca Sultanate. Dispersion of settlement made it inevitable that there should be a dispersed system of local control. In Negri Sembilan it had happened that such a decentralized system of district government had developed before there was any organ of central government at all; as a result the royal ruler was not only powerless but he governed under a constitution which was designed to yield that result. Perak and Selangor on the other hand had begun with a royal ruler and a concentration of power around that ruler in the tradition of the Malacca Sultanate. In these two States as the Malay population increased and scattered, an inevitable decentralization of authority began. Such was the prestige of the Malacca political system however that this decentralization of power was obliged to preserve the forms of central autocracy.

Chinese tin-mining as well as Malay immigration tended to produce a dispersal of power. So long as taxes on trade were the mainstay of government revenues, a Sultan residing at the mouth of the main river of the State might be able to collect more revenues than his chiefs and thus be stronger than they were. Chinese tin-mining however produced a source of revenue which could be tapped by local control.

A detailed account of dynastic history and civil war in the Malay States in the mid-nineteenth century must now be given.

PERAK

Perak had existed as a Malay State for several centuries. A process of disintegration, associated with mining development, began about 1850.

During the 1850's there was a civil war between the Sultan and certain of his chiefs. In this fighting the Sultan's son, Raja Yusuf, and a member of the Laxamana lineage, Mat Amin, particularly distinguished themselves. In 1857 the Sultan died. The Perak political system provided that in normal circumstances the Sultan should be succeeded by the Raja Muda; the Raja Bendahara became Raja Muda; the late Sultan's son became Raja Bendahara[1]. Each Sultan's son, if he lived long enough, would become Sultan after members of the two other branches of the royal lineage had had their turn. This system was only two generations old in 1850 and it was by no means fixed and unalterable. On the death of a Sultan it rested with the chiefs to decide how to fill the three royal offices.

In 1857 the Raja Muda, an opponent of the late Sultan, acceded as Sultan Ja'afar. The former Raja Bendahara became Raja Muda Ali. Thus far according to norm. But the chiefs refused to appoint the late Sultan's son, Raja Yusuf, to the vacant office of Raja Bendahara. He was personally

[1] See below, p. 62.

unpopular, he had fought against many of them in the recent civil war, and he was likely to be an autocratic Sultan later on. The chiefs therefore appointed one Raja Ismail to be Bendahara. Ismail was a member of the royal lineage only through his mother. It is probable that there was no intention at that time of promoting Ismail from Bendahara to Raja Muda and then to Sultan. He was merely a stop-gap to keep out Yusuf.

Sultan Ja'afar appointed Mat Amin to the office of Laxamana. In this capacity Mat Amin was the most powerful chief in lower Perak for the next twenty years. Another new family was rising to prominence. One Long Ja'afar had been appointed about 1840 to collect taxes for his kinsman, the Dato' Panglima Bukit Gantang, in the sparsely settled and remote areas of Krian and Larut. Tin was found at Larut and Long Ja'afar imported Chinese tin miners to work these deposits. The mines were a great success and Long Ja'afar became immensely wealthy. He died in 1857 and was succeeded by his son, Ngah Ibrahim (incidentally the prefix *Ngah* indicates that he was not the eldest son). In 1862 Ngah Ibrahim was given the title of Mentri, previously held by another lineage then in decline. As Mentri, Ngah Ibrahim ranked as one of the four chiefs of the first rank in Perak. He is always referred to as 'Mentri of Larut'; more correctly he was Mentri (Secretary of State) of Perak and incidentally chief of Larut. His case illustrates how the titles of office of the State Government had become associated with local chieftainships. The Mentri was related to the chiefs of upstream Perak, around Kuala Kangsar, and he became the leading member of that local group.

In 1865 Sultan Ja'afar died. Raja Muda Ali, a nonentity, was duly promoted to be Sultan. Raja Bendahara Ismail, not being truly royal, was left as Bendahara. Raja Abdullah, son of the late Sultan Ja'afar, was appointed direct to the vacant office of Raja Muda.

In the late 1860's the weakness of the Sultan left the chiefs without any focus of central control. They divided into two opposing local groups. Raja Bendahara Ismail, who had a substantial interest in the tin mines of Kinta, and the Mentri of Larut, which was an important mining district, were the leaders of the upstream group. Laxamana Mat Amin and Raja Muda Abdullah led the downstream group. Mat Amin, in partnership with the late Sultan Ja'afar, Abdullah's father, had opened up the mining district of Batang Padang. The division between these two groups was still spanned by kinship ties. The Mentri was a son-in-law of the Laxamana. Raja Muda Abdullah was a son-in-law of Sultan Ali, himself of the upstream group.

Sultan Ali died in 1871 in his village in upstream Perak. There was the usual meeting of chiefs to conduct the funeral and to elect a new Sultan. Custom required that the new Sultan should be present to preside over the funeral of his predecessor. Raja Muda Abdullah did not dare to go up-river among the hostile upstream chiefs; moreover he had lost face among them by his acquiescence in the abduction of his wife by one of their number. In his absence the Mentri persuaded the chiefs to appoint Raja Bendahara Ismail as Sultan. The immediate purpose was to install an ally as Sultan. It was also believed that the Mentri was intriguing for his own ultimate succession to the Sultanate. Ismail was elderly and not of royal descent on his father's side. When he died there would be a useful precedent in the Mentri's favour.[1]

Thereafter there were two contenders for recognition as Sultan. Ismail, though not of true royal descent, had been constitutionally elected by a majority of the chiefs of Perak. Abdullah, with a better title by descent and by having been the Raja Muda of the previous reign, laid claim to be Sultan with the support of Laxamana Mat Amin and the downstream chiefs.

In 1872 serious fighting broke out among two factions of Chinese miners at Larut. The Mentri, originally committed to the Hai San men, gave his support to whichever side seemed to be winning at the time. This policy was an indication of the essential weakness of his position; he had failed to use his resources to build up an adequate police to enforce his authority. Fortunes fluctuated in the fighting at Larut and the Mentri soon lost by his turncoat policy whatever influence he had had with either Chinese faction. At the beginning of 1873 he was driven out of the Chinese mining area of Larut and took refuge in the northern Malay area of Larut around Kurau and Krian. Abdullah, who recognized that the Mentri was the mainstay of the upstream coalition of his enemies, tried to dislodge him from Larut altogether.

Early in 1874 Sir Andrew Clarke, Governor of the Straits Settlements, intervened in Perak. Clarke and his advisers had only an imperfect understanding of the complicated succession dispute and the factors underlying it. Abdullah agreed to accept a British protectorate in Perak if the British would make him Sultan. The Mentri was forced to accept Abdullah as Sultan as a condition of being allowed to hold his district of Larut. The position of Sultan Ismail was left undetermined. The British were at this time unaware of the claims of Raja Yusuf, who had been appointed Raja Muda by Abdullah when he himself claimed to be Sultan.

The first British Resident of Perak, J. W. W. Birch, encountered much passive opposition in his attempts to introduce central collection of revenues in Perak and to abolish debt-bondage. Adversity reunited the factions among the Perak chiefs in opposition to Birch. In November 1875 Birch was murdered at Pasir Salak, village of the Maharaja Lela. After a punitive expedition ('the Perak War') had encountered little opposition, there was an enquiry into the origins of the attack on Birch. Sultan Abdullah, ex-Sultan Ismail, the Mentri and the Laxamana were all found to be implicated to a greater or less degree and they were exiled to the Seychelles. The only notability who was not in the plot was the ever-unpopular Raja Yusuf. Raja Bendahara Osman, son of the late

[1] Swettenham (1895), p. 202.

Sultan Ali, was mentally unstable and he died in 1876. The only other Malay chief of consequence was Raja Idris, cousin of Sultan Abdullah; his complicity in the events of 1875 was slight and he was not exiled.

In 1877 Raja Yusuf was appointed 'Regent' of Perak, *faute de mieux*, because the Anglo-Malay Treaty of 1874 postulated the existence of a Malay ruler of Perak whom the British would advise. Yusuf remained 'substantively' Raja Muda until 1886 when he was recognized as Sultan. He died in 1887. Raja Idris (or Dris) became Raja Bendahara in 1876 and Raja Muda in 1886. He succeeded Yusuf as Sultan Idris (1887–1916). From 1877 to 1889 Hugh Low was British Resident of Perak.

SELANGOR

The ruling dynasty of Selangor were a branch of a Bugis family established at Rhio, south of Singapore. Sultan Ibrahim, second Sultan of Selangor, died in 1826 leaving no son by his royal consort. He was eventually succeeded by Sultan Mohamed, a son by a secondary wife.

Sultan Mohamed was an ineffectual ruler. He tried to develop tin-mining in Selangor and in the course of these ventures he lost large sums of money borrowed from merchants in Malacca. In 1839, while on a journey between Selangor and Rhio, he was unwise enough to stop at Malacca. His creditors threatened him with arrest for debt. Raja Juma'at, a nephew of the Sultan's wife, rescued him from this predicament by taking over responsibility for the Sultan's debts (some £35,000). Raja Juma'at and his father, Raja Ja'afar, were members of the Rhio branch of the family. They had however begun to open tin-mines at Lukut, the southernmost of the five valleys of Selangor. In return for his assistance Raja Juma'at obtained from the Sultan a grant of the district of Lukut. He thus became a district chief with a title to Lukut instead of being merely a tin-miner in no man's land. Raja Juma'at consolidated his position by marrying a daughter of Sultan Mohamed. His brother Raja Abdullah married another daughter of the Sultan[1] or (according to other sources) a niece of the Sultan. But the two brothers, Juma'at and Abdullah, were still regarded as outsiders from Rhio by the Selangor-born aristocracy.

In 1853 a son of Sultan Mohamed, Raja Sulaiman, died. He had been chief of the Klang district but had failed to develop it satisfactorily. Sultan Mohamed passed over the claims of Raja Mahdi, son of Raja Sulaiman, to inherit his father's district and assigned Klang to Raja Abdullah, brother of Raja Juma'at. By this time Raja Juma'at had become wealthy from the rapidly increasing revenues of tin-mining at Lukut and, being wealthy, he was powerful. Raja Mahdi had perforce to accept the position.

Another prominent figure of this period was Raja Abdul Samad, a nephew and also a son-in-law of Sultan Mohamed. Abdul Samad had

[1] Winstedt (1934a).

financed tin-mining in the valley of the Selangor River with fair success.

Sultan Mohamed died in 1857. His eight-year old son, Raja Mahmud, had been appointed Raja Muda (at the insistence of the boy's mother) and was thus designated to succeed to the throne. Raja Juma'at however secured the succession for Raja Abdul Samad. The explanation was that Raja Juma'at, although the patrilineal grandson of a Sultan of Rhio, had no line of descent from the Selangor royal dynasty. Raja Abdul Samad, patrilineal grandson of Sultan Ibrahim of Selangor, was at least eligible to succeed. He and Raja Juma'at were brothers-in-law, both having married daughters of Sultan Mohamed; Raja Abdullah of Klang made a third of the trio of brothers-in-law. Sultan Abdul Samad, Raja Juma'at and Raja Abdullah between them controlled the greater part of Selangor.

The predominance of this coalition was much resented by the kinsmen of the late Sultan. In 1864 Raja Juma'at died and the coalition lost its most forceful member. In 1866 Raja Mahdi succeeded in driving Raja Abdullah out of Klang. Sultan Abdul Samad tried to remain neutral in this quarrel since so many of the Selangor aristocrats sympathized with Raja Mahdi. The Sultan had recently married his daughter to Tunku Kudin, the able and ambitious brother of the Sultan of Kedah. Tunku Kudin was appointed 'Viceroy' (*Wakil Yam Tuan*), possibly at his own request, with the task of settling the quarrel over Klang. By this manoeuvre Sultan Abdul Samad avoided committing his shaky personal authority to the support of either side and he provided a newcomer to the scene, linked with neither faction, as an arbitrator. The scheme failed because the Selangor aristocrats who backed Raja Mahdi were set on getting rid of outsiders. They had driven a Rhio chief out of Klang; they did not want to exchange him for a Viceroy from Kedah. The Mahdi faction denied the authority of Tunku Kudin who was forced into alliance with the sons of Raja Abdullah (Abdullah himself had died). Kudin had friends and backers among the business men of Singapore and Malacca; with their aid he was able to raise mercenary forces. He also found a powerful ally in Yap Ah Loy, the leader of the Chinese miners of Kuala Lumpur, and in the last stages of the civil war (1866–1873) he obtained help from the ruler of Pahang. Raja Mahdi was the acknowledged leader of the other side but there were two other leaders of almost equal prestige, Raja Mahmud and Syed Mashhor. Mashhor, an Arab half-caste, was by far the ablest general of the three. Mahdi, Mahmud and Mashhor were all nephews of Sultan Abdul Samad.

Lukut, under a son of Raja Juma'at, had sunk into a decline and played no part in the war.

In 1874 Selangor came under British protection. The British recognized Tunku Kudin as Viceroy. Sultan Abdul Samad reigned until 1898.

NEGRI SEMBILAN

During the seventeenth and eighteenth centuries the Malay immigrants from Menangkabau who had settled in Negri Sembilan gave some help to the Sumatran side in the intermittent wars between Sumatran chiefs, the Bugis of Rhio and the Dutch at Malacca. About 1760 the Bugis over-ran Sungei Ujong, a district of Negri Sembilan. They were soon driven out. But this reverse may have contributed to the decision of the Negri Sembilan chiefs to obtain a war-leader for the State. Up to that time they had had no higher political leadership other than unsuccessful pretenders and they merely acknowledged a vague tradition of suzerainty by the Sultans of Johore as successors to the Sultans of Malacca. The name 'Negri Sembilan' means 'Nine States' and indicates a group of small, independent districts.

The new leader was Raja Melewar, a member of the royal house of the Sumatran kingdom of Menangkabau. He was given only limited authority and revenues. The first three holders of the office (Yam Tuan of Negri Sembilan) were appointed for life; when each died a successor was invited over from Menangkabau. The second and third of these foreign princes married the daughter of his predecessor. A royal dynasty, patrilineal by sentiment, was thus built up by foreigners marrying into the matrilineal family of the district chief of Ulu Muar, in whose territory the royal ruler had his capital.

The sons of these unions naturally aspired to succeed to the throne. In the first quarter of the nineteenth century it was settled by the arbitrament of a civil war that sons of former rulers should succeed their fathers. Between about 1830 and 1860 the office of Yam Tuan was held by a forceful ruler, Yam Tuan Radin. He was unable, however, to make the authority of his office effective outside the limits of the royal domain. The threat of foreign attack receded and the development of tin-mining provided new bones of contention. The chiefs of Negri Sembilan and the Yam Tuan lived in an intermittent state of warfare with each other. Princes of the royal family penetrated into outlying districts of the State and tried to carve out districts for themselves by fighting or by marrying the daughters of chiefs. The complications of marriages between patrilineal royal princes of the paramount dynasty and women of the matrilineal clans from which the chiefs were drawn became obvious. Before the middle of the nineteenth century the matrilineal clans of Negri Sembilan had ceased to permit royal princes to marry their women. Thereafter the royal house was more or less endogamous.

The four major chiefs of Negri Sembilan were the *Undangs* (Lawgivers) of the districts of Sungei Ujong, Rembau, Jelebu and Johol. A branch of the royal house was established in the district of Tampin. There were two minor districts of Inas and Gemencheh attached to Johol; there was a district of Linggi colonized by Bugis who owed a vague allegiance to Sungei Ujong. Sungei Ujong itself was virtually divided in two because the Dato' Shahbandar held half the district in open defiance of the Undang of the whole of Sungei Ujong. The Yam Tuan's authority was limited to the four small districts of Terachi, Ulu Muar, Gunong Pasir and Jempol around the royal capital at Sri Menanti.

In 1860 Yam Tuan Radin died and was succeeded by his brother, Yam Tuan Imam. In 1869 Yam Tuan Imam died. There was then a long-drawn dispute between a son of Radin, Tunku Antah, and a son of Imam, Tunku Ahmad Tunggal. Tunku Antah had the support of most of the chiefs but his rival, Tunku Ahmad Tunggal, was backed by the Dato' Klana of Sungei Ujong, senior member of the college of the four chiefs of the first rank (the Undang). The Dato' Klana himself was not strongly established in Sungei Ujong and had difficulty in holding his own against the Dato' Shahbandar. In 1874 the Dato' Klana accepted British protection. The Dato' Shahbandar rose in revolt and was defeated by a British force. In 1875 Tunku Antah, now generally recognized as Yam Tuan, invaded Sungei Ujong. He was defeated and went into exile. He was restored in 1877 but only as overlord of the group of small districts around the royal capital. The major chiefs no longer acknowledged him as paramount.

Until 1886 only Sungei Ujong was under British protection though British administrators frequently visited other districts of Negri Sembilan and sometimes mediated in the many quarrels between the chiefs. The whole state came under British protection about 1887. In 1898 the position of the Yam Tuan as paramount ruler of the entire state was again acknowledged by all the chiefs.

PAHANG

Originally Pahang had been an outlying province of the Johore Sultanate ruled by a more or less independent but non-royal chief, with the title of Bendahara of Pahang. As the Johore Sultanate lapsed into impotence in the seventeenth and eighteenth centuries the independence and the pretensions of the rulers of Pahang increased.

In 1857 the Bendahara of Pahang died and was succeeded by his eldest son. Another son, Ahmad, rose in revolt against the legitimate ruler. The civil war ended in 1863 with the victory of Ahmad. He was a forceful leader and in the course of the war he had built up a strong following and had weakened his opponents among the chiefs. He came to the throne with much greater power than his contemporaries among the rulers of the other States. Moreover there was much less tin-mining in Pahang than in the other three States already described. The ruling class as a group was poorer in consequence but the Bendahara was relatively richer and therefore more powerful.

There was nonetheless a good deal of tension between the Bendahara and the chiefs. In 1882 the Bendahara assumed the title of Sultan. The discontents of the chiefs had been focused in support of the Raja Muda, a brother of the Sultan and at one time a trusted supporter. Raja Muda Mansor resented the Sultan's unwillingness to give him a larger share of the royal revenues and his evident intention to arrange for the succession after his death of his son rather than his brother, the Raja Muda. There was a certain amount of British mediation. Swettenham visited Pahang in 1885. In 1887 Hugh Clifford was appointed 'British Agent'. In 1888 the Sultan was prevailed upon to accept British protection.

In the context of social anthropology the Malay States are unusual in that their history is known with fair accuracy for some centuries back. It is thus possible to attempt an assessment of the contribution which a knowledge of the previous history of a society can make to the analysis of its social institutions. A distinction must of course be made between history proper (knowledge of what actually happened) and myth and tradition (what people *now* say happened in the past). The latter is an obvious element in the current situation. In so far as tradition is bad history and gives a false picture of the past, it must be distinguished from history.

There is, in any culture, much which cannot be explained in terms of structure and function, of inevitable regularities imposed by the circumstances of the present time and of social needs to be met. There is always a wide field besides of optional or variable behaviour, especially in the sphere of aesthetic expression, but in much else also. In part this optional element is to be explained as the sphere of individual choice. But there is more to it than that. Much of it is not, in the present generation at least, the result of individual creation, choice or initiative. It is entirely socialized, the common property of all.

The explanation lies in the fact that no generation of a society begins with a clean slate. No doubt it must order its affairs and satisfy its needs in accordance with the circumstances of its own era—and these circumstances may be different from those of the generation before. But, except in situations of migration and abrupt culture contact, there is rarely the possibility, still less the inclination, to jettison all that was done before. Even a Nyakusa age grade assuming control for the first time is habituated to a system in which Nyakusa age grades are a fundamental institution.[1] The attitude of the rising generation to the practices and values of its elders is perhaps ambivalent, a mixture of respect and revolt. But there is always sufficient inclination to preserve some at least of the traditions of the past. This is so because a society cannot exist without a texture of common culture—and this cannot be wholly invented in a short time. The tendency therefore is for each generation to preserve, and to esteem

[1] G. Wilson (1951).

the preservation of, the practices of their predecessors. If there are new or modified social needs, they are more likely to be met by an adaptation of an old institution than by the invention of a new one. The form is thus continued when the function changes. The form, provided its perpetuation unchanged is not allowed to confuse the identification of new functions, is an element in the total social situation and can generally be best understood by reference to its history. It is often inexplicable without a knowledge of its history. Such a case was the preservation of the old offices of state of the Malacca Sultanate to serve as district chieftainships in the late nineteenth century Malay States. One can demonstrate that the circumstances of that latter period required an institution such as the chieftainship of a district with the structural features which it possessed. But the reason why such an institution was associated with the use of irrelevant titles (such as 'Laxamana'—an admiral who never went to sea), with ceremonial dignities around the person of the Sultan which imposed conduct in conflict with the real feelings of the chief towards the Sultan, and with gradations of status between chiefs—all this is hardly to be explained without knowing the history of the matter. Moreover this pursuit of the origins of the outward form of institutions may eventually bring the enquirer round in full circle back to the analysis of structure and function in the current situation. The more intangible elements of culture, the attitudes, values and sentiments underlying the outward forms of conduct seem (it is at least an hypothesis) to persist for longer periods than purely functional analysis would justify, by virtue of an inherent quality of their own. This fact, it is suggested, is related to the preference for preserving the habits of the past, these being (until something better can be devised) the means by which the group holds together in distinction from outsiders.[1]

FOREIGN INFLUENCE

Earlier passages have mentioned incidentally the impact of alien political, commercial and cultural influences on the Malays. It is worth summarizing this aspect of the situation for it was important.

The key to the matter is that the Malay Peninsula, more especially its west coast, lies on one of the most ancient and most important trade routes in the world. It is known that there were a series of trade links between the Roman Empire, India and China. One sea-route from India to China passed down the Straits of Malacca. Trade, conquest and religious proselytization seem to go hand in hand in such cases.

It thus happened that Malay settlements of a thousand years ago or more were dependencies of Indian, Annamite, Sumatran and Javanese kingdoms and absorbed into their political ideology the forms and structures of those kingdoms. At a later period the Malay rulers of five hundred

[1] See below, p. 134.

years ago were in nominal subjection to Siam and China. With the coming of the Portuguese in 1509 the Malays began a continuing contact with the European powers. Until the nineteenth century it was a relationship of trade and warfare. Then began the more pervasive economic and political influence of the Pax Britannica extended to a 'sphere of influence' in the Malay Peninsula.

The Malay economy was by no means a closed and self-sufficient system. The export of tin provided the means of buying cloth, foodstuffs and other necessaries from abroad. As a consequence of this foreign trade the Malay economy was based on a monetary system of exchange. There is, for example, no common Malay word for 'barter'. It is not suggested that all economic exchanges were by payment in money. Wealth was more often accumulated in tin ingots than in coin. There had at one time been an indigenous system of tin coinage (before the nineteenth century) but at the period with which this study is concerned almost everything which had an exchange value was expressed in terms of dollars.[1] It was this habit of valuation in monetary terms which was significant. Actual payments were often in kind; e.g. *ad valorem* taxes on commerce were sometimes collected by appropriation of a due proportion of the goods.

The Malays had originally shared the Indonesian heritage of pagan belief and ritual. Much of this element survived in their culture under the overlay of universal religions. During their period of subjection to Hindu kingdoms the Malays had been Hindus. Elements of Hinduism persisted in much of the ritual around the throne of Malay States, in dramatic and pictorial art and in Malay demonology. About 1400 A.D. the Malays became converts to Islam, absorbing with this new creed elements of the south Indian and north Sumatran cultures through which Islam came to them. Malay absorption of Islam was selective and incomplete at this period.

A GENERAL PICTURE OF THE MALAY POLITICAL SYSTEM

As an introduction to the detailed description in subsequent sections of this book it may be useful to describe in outline the main features of the Malay political system viewed as a whole. Any such account in general terms must to some extent be an abstraction and simplification which ceases to correspond exactly with the complicated facts of the situation. It may serve however to show the shape of the wood before coming to the trees.

---

[1] The 'Mexican dollar' was, in the nineteenth century, a silver coin valued at about five dollars to the pound sterling according to the world price of silver. The dollar was the currency of the British—administered Straits Settlements. There was no current indigenous Malay coinage.

The largest political unit was the State. The Malay word for State is *Negri* (used as a classificatory prefix—e.g. *Negri Perak, Negri Selangor*, &c.). Significantly, in view of the derivation of the Malay political system from the Malacca Sultanate, *negri* meant originally a city. By the nineteenth century however *negri* generally denoted an extent of territory under an independent ruler.

The territory comprised in a State was related to the geographical structure of the peninsula and to the use of rivers as the main lines of communication and trade. A State was typically the basin of a large river or (less often) of a group of adjacent rivers, forming a block of land extending from the coast inland to the central watershed. The capital of the State was the point at which the main river ran into the sea. At this point the ruler of the State could control the movement of all persons who entered or left his State, he could defend it from external attack and he could levy taxes on its imports and exports.

The apex of the State as a political unit was its ruler who was drawn from a royal patrilineage and invested with attributes of supernatural power and dignity. He bore the title *Yang di-Pertuan Besar* (He who is made lord). In most cases he bore the Arabic personal honorific prefix *Sultan* (which in Arabic denotes an independent ruler). The functions of the royal ruler were to exercise the limited powers of central government, to conduct external relations, to provide leadership in foreign wars and to embody and symbolize the unity and welfare of the state. He was assisted and supported by his kinsmen in the royal lineage and by a number of executive assistants.

In descending order of size the next political unit was the district (*jajahan* or *daerah*). Like the State the district was a territory shaped by the use of rivers as communications. A district was either an area lying on one or both sides of a reach of the main river of the State or it was a side valley down to the point of junction with the main stream. A fort at the downstream end of the district provided an effective means of control.

The ruler of a district was a chief drawn from a lineage which usually had a long-established connexion with the district. In addition to their local connexion with one district each, the lineages of chiefs also formed a more or less united ruling class of the whole State. As will appear later, there was considerable variation between States in respect of chieftainships. Some chiefs were drawn from the royal lineage, more especially from cadet branches which no longer had any serious prospect of providing a candidate for succession to the throne. More typically however chiefs came from non-royal but aristocratic lineages.

The existence of a ruling class was one of the most important elements of the political system. The division between ruling class and subject class was a political alignment which was rarely bridged by intermarriage or the advancement of a member of the subject class to the ruling class. The term for the subject class was *ra'ayat* (both for an individual and for the class collectively).[1] There was no comprehensive term for the ruling class.[2] The word *Raja* (a ruler) or *anak raja* (son of a ruler or princeling) could be applied by way of description to those members of either sex of the ruling class who were of royal patrilineal descent. The prefix *Raja* or *Tunku* was used as an honorific prefix to their names. But *Raja* could not be applied to a chief, however exalted, of non-royal descent. Such a non-royal chief bore a special title of office and he was addressed and referred to as *Dato'* (grandfather or chief). There was no all-inclusive term for members of the ruling class who were not chiefs and were not of royal descent. Close relatives of a chief however sometimes bore the personal prefix *Wan* before their names. These niceties are connected with the all-pervasive conception of differential status in the ruling class.

The functions of a chief in his district were local administration, justice, defence, revenue collection and general leadership. The chief had few ritual functions. He was assisted by a number of helpers and deputies who were generally close kinsmen.

The smallest political unit was the village (*kampong*). This was a unit of common residence and, to some extent, of kinship and economic co-operation. Only secondarily was it a unit of political control. The head of the village (except in Negri Sembilan) was the *Penghulu* (headman) who was the bridge and channel of communication between his group of villagers and the district chief. The *Penghulu*, although he enjoyed high status within his village was generally of the subject class.

The following chapter describes the Malay village community as a residential, economic and social unit. Some description of the governed seems a necessary preliminary to an account of the system of government. The latter is obviously adapted to the former and cannot be explained in isolation from it.

---

[1] Arabic, 'subject of a ruler'. Cf. the Indian form *ryot*.

[2] The absence of a specific term for a recognized group is apparently not significant. Cf. Nadel (1951), p. 148. 'It may simply not be important for the people to demonstrate their unity by the special pointer of a name if that unity is sufficiently visible in their co-activities or in their formulated codes and statutes.'

2

The Malay Village Community

POPULATION

There was no comprehensive census of the population of Perak, Selangor and Negri Sembilan until 1891.[1] The 1891 census figures are useless as a guide to the population of twenty years before because there was a very rapid growth of population by unrecorded immigration during the 1880's. It was said of Malay chiefs in the 1870's that they were quite ignorant 'of the numbers of the settled, wandering and floating population of their districts'.[2] The estimates of European observers must therefore be treated with caution. Moreover the population tended to run away whenever the fighting of the civil wars of the 1870 period came near their villages. Sometimes they returned when the fighting was over but sometimes they made new homes elsewhere. The population therefore fluctuated a great deal.

McNair estimated the Malay population of Perak in 1870 at 30,000.[3] A count for poll-tax purposes in 1879 gave a total of 31,553.[4] The Malay population of Selangor, much depleted by seven years of civil war, was estimated in 1874 at 5,000; by 1878 it was estimated to have increased to 10,000. A rough census of 1884 showed the Malay population of Selangor as 17,097.[5] The Malay population of Negri Sembilan was of the order of 30,000 to 40,000.[6]

The Chinese population fluctuated even more sharply than the Malay

[1] The 1891 census figures were:

State	Malays and Malaysians	Others*	Total
Perak	106,393	107,861	214,254
Selangor	26,578	55,014	81,592
Negri Sembilan	48,480	22,250	70,730

* predominantly Chinese

[2] McNair (1878), p. 156.　　　[3] McNair, (1887), p. 157.　　　[4] *AR Pk*, 1888.

[5] 1874: *SSD*, 27 April 1875; 1878: *SSD*, 6 March 1879; 1884: *AR Sel*, 1884.

[6] The Malay population of Sungei Ujong district was estimated at 2,000 in 1878 (*SSD*, 6 March 1879); at the census of 1891 it was 9,341 (*AR SU*, 1891). The Malay population of Jelebu district was estimated at 2,000 in 1891 (*AR Jelebu*, 1891). The Malay population of the rest of Negri Sembilan (apart from Sungei Ujong and Jelebu) was estimated at 30,000 in 1888 (*AR NS*, 1888). Of this total of 30,000 some 10,000 were in the Rembau district (Swettenham 1880).

owing to sudden changes in the fortunes of mining camps in ore extraction and in warfare. At Larut, the main mining centre in Perak, the Chinese population was estimated at 40,000 in 1871, 4,000 in January 1874, 27,000 in December 1874, 15,000 in 1876 and 9,000 in 1877; a rough count in 1879 gave a total of 16,953.[1]

At Kuala Lumpur, the main mining centre of Selangor, the Chinese mining population was estimated at 10,000 in 1870, 5,000 in 1873 and 20,000 in 1879; at the count of 1884 it was returned as 28,236.[2] Lukut, once an important mining centre in Selangor had dwindled from 2,000 in 1870 to 300 in 1874. The Chinese population of Sungei Ujong in Negri Sembilan was estimated at 10,000 in 1874 and 6,000 in 1878.[3]

There were many other smaller local groups of Chinese miners. But miners moved from one place to another. Thus it is known that at different times there were quite large movements from Larut and from Sungei Ujong to Kuala Lumpur. The figures are unreliable and any attempt to arrive at totals runs the risk of double counting if figures are taken from different places in different years.

In the context of a study of the Malay political system it is more useful to divide Chinese mining communities into categories differentiated by the degree of Malay control. Large mining centres such as Larut, Kuala Lumpur and Lukut (in its heyday) were beyond the administrative resources of Malay chiefs to control. The chiefs, standing between the mines and the sea, could usually levy export duties on tin but could rarely interfere in the internal affairs of the mining communities. In the smaller centres where there were only a few hundred miners the local Malay chiefs might be able to exercise some general control and even to participate as sleeping partners in the profits of the mines. Finally there were cases of Malay chiefs who employed Chinese miners in small numbers under their own management.

Whenever there was any considerable number of Chinese it was found convenient to have a headman (bearing the title *Capitan China* conferred on him by the Malay ruler). This headman was of course always a Chinese

[1] 1871: *SSD*, 3 August 1879; 1874: *SSD*, 6 April 1875; 1876: *SSD*, 24 April 1876 ('at a low estimate 15,000 Chinese'); 1877: *SSD*, of 1877 or 1878 the particulars of which I failed to note; 1879: *AR Pk*, 1888. On the Larut Chinese population question see Gullick (1953b), p. 49.

[2] See Middlebrook (1951). Other figures are 12,000 in 1872 (*SSD*, 6 November 1872); 20,000 in 1878 (*SSD*, 6 March 1879); 16,000 in 1878 (*SSD*, 1 August 1878).

[3] 1874: *SSD*, 29 December, 1874; 1878: *SSD*, 6 March 1879. Pickering (*SSD*, 24 April 1876) put the Chinese population at 10,000 in 1876. There is some difficulty in reconciling these figures. The 1874 figure of 10,000 was given by Pickering, a Chinese Affairs expert who had been there. Swettenham (*SSD*, 6 March 1878) after his visit of 1878 reported that the population had decreased by 40 per cent since 1874. The inference is that there were 6,000 Chinese in Sungei Ujong in 1878. Yet Swettenham in the same report gives a combined Malay and Chinese figure of 5,000 only.

and was usually the leading mine manager of the centre. The Malay ruling class thus dealt with the Chinese as groups rather than as individuals. The Malay peasants had comparatively little to do with Chinese miners. The Chinese population consisted almost entirely of adult males who intended to return to China eventually. It was thus unbalanced, impermanent and unstable.

The composition of the Malay population was extremely mixed. It appears that the majority were of Menangkabau birth or descent.[1] In Negri Sembilan the whole social system was a modified version of the Menangkabau model. In Perak the local-born Malays accepted Menangkabau immigrants, but no others, as kindred to themselves.[2] There were however many other elements. In Perak in addition to local-born Malays and Menangkabau immigrants there were Bugis (from the Celebes), Korinchi, Rawa, Mandiling and Batak men from Sumatra.[3] In Selangor the peasantry were a mixture of Batak, Rawa and Mandiling groups (especially the latter). Even in predominantly Menangkabau Negri Sembilan there was at least one Bugis colony (at Linggi) and the Rawa traders had been numerous enough in 1848 to give their name to a civil war. The names of the Negri Sembilan clans also indicate that some members of the Malay community were descended from immigrants of Malacca, Javanese and Achehnese origin. The Arabs who intermarried with the Malays were a small but influential group in the spheres of trade and religion. Many of these 'Arabs' were of no more than mixed Arab/Achehnese descent.

The different elements in the Malay population, despite their participation in a general Indonesian culture, were extremely conscious of their differences. The Bugis in Perak spoke their own language and rarely intermarried with other Malaysians[4]. The Korinchi claimed to be stricter Muslims than other Malaysians. They wore all white clothing and held themselves aloof from the rest.[3] In Selangor there was a tradition of hostility between the Bugis aristocracy and the Sumatran miners and peasants of recent immigrant origin. The Selangor chiefs dealt with this element among their subjects by the appointment of 'headmen of foreigners' (*Dato' Dagang*) as intermediaries. In Negri Sembilan the Menangkabau Malays at various times expelled the Bugis and the Rawa traders.

These half-subdued dislikes found expression in many ways besides occasional fighting. In addition to deliberate differences of dress and language there were also occupational lines of cleavage. Indonesian immigrants seem to have kept local trade in their own hands (friction on this score was said to have been the origin of the Rawa War of 1848 in Negri Sembilan). They formed a large part of the retinues of armed men

[1] Menangkabau was a kingdom in the Padang Highlands of Sumatra, noted for its matrilineal social system.

[2] McNair (1878), pp. 130 ff.   [3] McNair, loc. cit.   [4] McNair, loc. cit.

C

around the chiefs. By contrast local-born Malays of the commoner class were more often peasants. Even where the immigrants were settled as peasants, the cleavage persisted. Each village consisted of members of one cultural group and generally included no others. Even in 1892 it was noted that immigrants (*anak dagang*) would not deal with or settle near the longer established villages of local-born Malays (*anak negri*).[1]

These contrasts and conflicts between groups within the Malay community were of some political significance. It was a situation in which the Malay ruling class could to some extent play the game of 'divide and rule'. A chief with a retinue of foreign-born Malays could count on their loyalty to help him over-awe his local-born subjects in their villages. Equally his followers could not hope to lead a general revolt against him. The consciousness of cultural differences and the hostility arising from it tended to weld the members of each homogeneous village group into a compact and partially endogamous body, loyal to its headman and through him more easily susceptible of control.

Most important of all however was the effect of these cultural differences on the very nature of the political system. It has been written of African tribes that 'Cultural and economic heterogeneity is associated with a state-like political structure. Centralized authority and an administrative organization seem to be necessary to accommodate culturally diverse groups within a single political system.'[2] Perak and Selangor at least seem to go some way to support this proposition. The situation in Negri Sembilan is discussed later in this chapter.[3]

On the assumption, which seems justified, that the major line of cleavage and hostility was between local-born Malays and immigrants, the question arises as to the numbers of each category. As a small but completely random example there is mention of a boatload of men travelling on the Perak River in 1874. Five men were Malays born in Perak, one came from Trengganu (in the north-east region of the Malay Peninsula), and the other three had been born in three different parts of Sumatra. It may be of course that foreign Malays were more likely to be found making a long journey. It is at least fairly certain that in the period around 1870 the large-scale Indonesian immigration which was so notable a phenomenon later on had not begun. Comparison of the 1870 population[4] and Newbold's figures for 1830 indicate that there was little gain from immigration up to 1870.[5] But there may have been much two-way movement. There is indeed no other way to reconcile the two facts that (*a*) the Malay population of 1870 was little larger than it had been in 1830 and (*b*) that

[1] *AR*, District Officer, Kuala Selangor, 1892.
[2] Fortes & Evans-Pritchard (1940).
[3] See below, p. 37.   [4] See above, p. 23.
[5] Newbold's figures quoted in the *Malayan Census Report* (1947) are Perak, 35,000; Selangor, 1,200; and Negri Sembilan, 27,680.

it undoubtedly included a considerable number of recent immigrants. The only other possible explanation would be abnormally high death rates of which there is no evidence.[1]

Another aspect of this question of the balance of local-born and immigrant population is the rate of absorption of immigrants into the recognized 'local Malay' community. Modern census work indicates that such absorption is above all a subjective process, i.e. the son or remoter descendant of an immigrant becomes a local-born Malay in the eyes of others when he is so in his own eyes (and he behaves accordingly).[2]

THE MALAY VILLAGE

The sparse Malay population of the 1870's lived in villages on the banks of rivers. This riverain pattern of settlement was dictated by the fact that the rivers were the only convenient communications. As an illustration of the significance of communications in the siting of settlements, British administrators in the 1880's noticed that as soon as a road was built, Malays began to build houses on the previously uninhabited land on either side of the road.[3] Malay villages were not economically self-sufficient. Their imports and exports had to come and go by river. The further inland they settled, the more toll-stations their goods must pass. Thus it was found in Pahang in the 1880's that essential imports cost twice as much in Ulu Pahang (the interior) as at the coast.[4] Thus there was an inducement to villagers to settle not only on the banks of rivers but also fairly near the sea. An additional reason was that good alluvial soil was more often found along the lower reaches of rivers.

The villages varied in size from hamlets of some five houses to large settlements of a hundred houses or more. In general each simple family of man, wife and children had its own house and the number of persons per house was probably about five on the average. All villages, large and small, were described by the word *kampong*, meaning a cluster or group.[5]

[1] The accurate recording of births and deaths began a generation later when the incipient government health services had already begun to affect mortality. Hence nothing can be inferred from them about the situation in 1870.

[2] Cf. Vlieland (1931): 'In the vast majority of cases the children of immigrant (Indonesian) parents become merged at once in the Malay population, and regard British Malaya as their country. In the case of the Javanese on the other hand, the process of absorption or subjective "naturalization" is much slower and commonly takes several generations, the determining factor frequently being intermarriage.'

[3] For example, *AR*, District Officer, Jelebu (Negri Sembilan), 1890: 'The tendency of these people is to build small houses along the sides of government roads.'

[4] *SSD*, 28 April 1887. A pound of Java tobacco cost 40–45 cents in Perak (where the toll system no longer obtained) but $1 in Ulu Pahang.

[5] *Kampong* can also be used in an adjectival or participial form to describe a collection of people. But the usage is rare and *kampong*, unless the context otherwise

Nonetheless a distinction was made between large and small villages. For some reason a minimum of forty houses was taken as the approximate criterion of a village large enough to have a headman of its own and a mosque with its complement of mosque officials.[1] A particularly large village was often the residence of a chief whose district included a number of other villages and hamlets in the neighbourhood in addition to his 'capital'. The Malay population of a district seems to have been of the order of 1,000 people. This number was perhaps the minimum more or less that could support a chief; but much depended on how large or small a revenue the chief obtained from trade goods passing through the district and from tin mines in the district.

The size and lay-out of the village was determined by the needs of village life. The river was the high-road, the water supply, the bath and the drain. It was more convenient to live on the river bank than anywhere else. The houses therefore were strung out in a line along the edge of the bank. In some cases there was a second line of houses further inland, separated from the first by a muddy lane. The houses were not evenly equidistant but tended to be grouped in clusters (for reasons to be explained hereafter).[2]

The optimum size of the village was limited by the availability of suitable land for rice cultivation. Dry rice could be grown on hillsides but the heavier-yielding wet padi, which was the staple foodcrop, required level and well-watered land. Malay padi cultivators relied mainly on rainwater for irrigation. They had only very limited technical ability for constructing irrigation works.[3] Moreover there were political disincentives to sinking capital in land by building irrigation dams and channels.[4] A village of 30–50 houses was in most cases as large a population as could find naturally suitable padi land within a convenient distance of the village site. Land elsewhere was abundant and free for the taking.[5] It was therefore

[1] McNair (1878), p. 228 and Wilkinson (1902), under *Mukim*.

[2] See below, p. 33.

[3] Clifford noted that Pahang Malays employed Kelantan men to build their irrigation channels (*AR Phg* 1891 and 1893). He attributed this to laziness— but *quaere*.

[4] See below, p. 29.

[5] Swettenham (1948), p. 136. 'Land had no value in the Malay States of 1874 and it was the custom for anyone to settle where he pleased on unoccupied and unclaimed land.' The situation in Negri Sembilan was rather different; see below p. 40.

requires, is always taken to mean a group of houses forming a village. The only word for town (other than the archaic use of *negri*, see p. 21 above) in the Malay States was *bandar*, meaning a port or harbour. *Bandar* was commonly used of the royal capital because it was a port on the coast. Thus Bandar near the mouth of the Perak River was the state capital of 1874. The capital of Selangor at the same period was Bandar Termasa at the mouth of the Langat River. No other large villages in either state were called *bandar*.

easy for a section of a big village to break away and found a new hamlet nearby.

Why then did the Malays congregate in villages at all instead of scattering in isolated homesteads where each could have the pick of the padi land? First, there were some countervailing advantages in having a large, continuous cultivated area. It was, for example, easier to keep out pests and weeds. Secondly, it was usual to construct ditches and banks on the landward side of villages to prevent buffaloes from straying into the fields while the padi was growing. These earthworks which were also used for local defence were more economically maintained by a larger group than the family. Thirdly, a large village, if it was the residence of a chief, would have a stockade as the main element in its defence, and also some shops. Finally, the chiefs preferred to keep their subjects in compact groups for ease of control.

The nature of Malay settlement and land use was much influenced by political factors. Malay settlement in the 1870's was consciously impermanent. Flight was a recognized response to hostile invasion or undue oppression. In the mid-nineteenth century both these evils were common. In 1892 Malays said:

'In former days there was nothing to eat, there being a dearth of buffaloes, the planting of padi was difficult, and no one could be certain that he would not have to fly on the morrow.'[1]

Selangor suffered particularly badly from depopulation due to the civil war of 1866–73. Twenty years later it was recorded:

'In the old Malay times before Selangor was upset by the struggles between rival Rajas, large crops of rice were raised in this district (Kuala Selangor) so much so that the supply far exceeded the demand, even in those days when the country was far more populous than it is now.'[2]

'The Selangor raiat disappeared in the troublous times of past years and is practically non-existent now.'[3]

The age when peasants grew more padi than was required for their own consumption ended before 1870. In the decade 1870–80 rice was habitually imported into Perak and Selangor and even, in years of poor harvests, into Negri Sembilan.[4]

In these circumstances few peasants were inclined to invest their labour in irrigation works to improve their land. Their other crops were not for the most part perennial. They included coffee, tobacco, sago, bananas, maize and sometimes sugar cane, tapioca, or pepper and gambier. Their tree crops were sugar palm, areca, betel, coconut, durian, mangosteen

[1] *AR NS*, 1892.

[2] Report by District Officer, Kuala Selangor, published in *Selangor Gazette* of 1893.

[3] *AR Sel*, 1904.

[4] *AR Sungei Ujong*, 1892, records that Jelebu Malays grew rice only for their own consumption and that rice for Chinese had to be imported. *AR NS*, 1901 and 1904, record fluctuations in rice imports due to bad and good harvests respectively.

and other fruits. But all these crops were grown only on a small scale and partly for domestic consumption. To have an evident surplus was to invite confiscation:

> 'The authorities, Sultan, State Officer, local headman or *anak raja*, whoever had the power of might . . . helped themselves to any produce that they thought worth having whenever they felt able and inclined.'[1]

Nor was there any inducement to sell produce to accumulate money:

> 'Few commoners accumulated any wealth; if they did so a Raja would rob them of it or oblige them to lend it without any prospect of repayment.'[2]

Their houses were flimsy structures of jungle poles and split bamboo matting with a palm thatch. Their household goods were few and portable; pandanus mats (*mengkuang*) in particular were usually taken if they were obliged to move.

The techniques of agricultural production did not dictate sustained economic co-operation on any wider scale than the family working group. There was no marked seasonal rhythm in their activities. But co-operation among villagers did occur here and there on a limited scale, e.g. a newly arrived settler had to clear land and bring it into production. During his first season or two he was often unable to support himself and his dependents from the yield of his own fields. In such cases his wealthier neighbours, especially the village headman, would help him out. It was a recognized practice for a headman to attract settlers to his village by offering such help in the early years of their residence. The debt was repaid in loyalty and service later on.

The existence of larger contiguous blocks of padi land than the holdings of individual families imposed a measure of concerted action. There are advantages in working land in such blocks:

> 'Isolated patches are more troublesome to manage, especially in regard to water-supply, more liable to damage by pests and more expensive to cultivate than larger areas.'[3]

But the advantages of a larger contiguous cultivated area are lost if there is no common timetable for planting operations. If each plants as he pleases, one will want the fields to be drained off for reaping while the padi of another is still green. Pests lurk in the plots of mature padi and sally forth to devastate the growing plants nearby. Despite these compelling reasons for concerting padi planting operations, there was great difficulty in imposing a common programme. The absence of any marked dry season left much discretion as to the best time for planting. Hugh Clifford records an interesting debate in the Pahang State Council:

> '. . . the chiefs strongly expressing the opinion that the cultivators were incapable of combining among themselves to agree to any such arrangement as

[1] Swettenham, *AR Pk*, 1890.

[2] Swettenham, *SSD*, 16 October 1875.

[3] A special report on the Agricultural Department published as an *F.M.S. Federal Council Paper* in 1919.

the simultaneous planting of their crops. . . . Selfish considerations, they said, would always lead some members of a village community to delay planting in spite of any mutual agreement; others, fearing the destruction of their crops by vermin if planted before those of their neighbours would follow this example . . . many years ago His Highness the Sultan issued an order that all crops should be planted simultaneously upon a fixed date.'[1]

This passage, if it describes a typical situation, indicates how very limited was the authority of village headmen. These headmen and the other leaders of the village had no force with which to compel obedience. They could however enforce a measure of concerted action through fixing the dates of the rituals of the padi planting cycle.

Sale of surplus foodstuffs or of cash crops, both on a very small scale, was the main source of income of the Malay peasant. The needs of Chinese mining communities for rice, etc. provided a ready market for anything he had to sell. He could also collect forest products such as damar, rattan, gutta percha and bamboo and sell it for export. Buffalo horns and hides were another exportable product. Few villagers were willing to work regularly for a wage. There was little demand for wage labour since chiefs could call on their subjects for unlimited free labour under a corvée system called *kerah*.[2] But occasional wage labour such as poling a boat on a journey provided the means of earning money. In inland villages trade was in the hands of Indonesian immigrants; it was not an occupation in which a peasant had much opportunity. In the larger centres there were a few Chinese shopkeepers.

The money which a peasant earned in these various ways was spent on the purchase of rice, salt, textiles and other necessaries.

There were few full-time craftsmen except in the retinue of Sultans and great chiefs. Only wealthy patrons could provide steady employment for a silversmith or a woodworker. Here and there was a village with a minor industry. There is a reference to a village of Korinchi (Mandiling) craftsmen near Kuala Kangsar in Perak who were famous for their knives; Sungei Siput nearby was known for its knives and spears.[3] There were however only six or seven craftsmen in the Korinchi village and it took them ninety days to fulfil an order for ten spears and twenty knives worth $125.

Craftsmen and like specialists enjoyed prestige by reason of their occupation. The explanation may be that in many cases their occupation brought them into close contact with the ruling class. Elephant mahouts, for example, were a respected class (elephants were royal mounts) and so were members of royal bands.

COMPOSITION OF THE VILLAGE GROUP

Very little is known of the composition of village communities in terms of

[1] *AR Phg*, 1897.   [2] See below, p. 108.   [3] Swettenham (1951), pp. 49–50.

kinship and social organization. What follows by way of description is based on rather scrappy evidence.

In Perak and Selangor there was apparently no uniform pattern (Negri Sembilan villages are described separately later[1]). In view of the impermanence of village settlement and the marked cultural differences between one village and another, the regularity and uniformity bred of long-established residence and social homogeneity is hardly to be looked for.

Nonetheless it is possible to trace certain general features of sufficient regularity to be regarded as structural. Many villages had no long tradition behind them. They had been founded within living memory. The original focus of each village settlement had been a founding family led by a headman. The same process was still at work in Selangor in the 1890's from whose administrative records the following incidental comments on new villages are taken:

> 'It would be a very good thing to settle some influential native at Batang Berjuntai and assist him with a loan to open the place.'[2]
>
> 'Che Mat, the headman of the Kelantan colony here [sc: at Sungei Buloh] has started for his country to collect padi planters who will settle on this newly opened land.'[3]

In these frontier conditions the founder and first headman of the village brought with him some of his kindred, by blood or affinity, and also attracted to his new settlement other recruits from his own home village or from the circle of his acquaintance. The attraction lay in his personal qualities as a leader, his ability and willingness to give new settlers economic assistance while they cleared land and brought crops to maturity and on his ties of kinship with them, either before they came to the new village or by subsequent intermarriage between his family and theirs. The strongest tie of all was common cultural origin, e.g. in the passage quoted above Che Mat was going from Selangor to Kelantan, a long and difficult journey across the peninsula, to recruit settlers from the State in which he had been born.

As has been said,[4] the size of villages varied considerably. A hamlet of half a dozen houses might consist only of a single group of kinsmen led by one of their senior members. A larger village would consist of the 'founder family' and several other separate groups of kinsfolk. Each of these groups of kinsfolk tended to live together in a cluster of houses closer to each other than to other groups of houses in the village. For convenience these 'clusters' are referred to hereafter as 'homesteads'; in Malay however the word *kampong* is used for a homestead as well as for a village made up of several homesteads.

If the village was large enough to be the residence of a chief, his household of fighting men, attendants, messengers, boatmen, concubines and

[1] See below, p. 37.

[2] Report by District Officer, Kuala Selangor in *Selangor Gazette* of 1892.

[3] *Selangor Gazette* of 1893.   [4] See above, p. 27.

handmaidens made up an additional element in the village. A large village might also include some shopkeepers and traders who might be outsiders to the village community proper.

There is very little evidence of the kinship ties which linked the kinsfolk who lived together in homesteads. There was apparently no set pattern. Swettenham throws some light on the matter in the following passage:

'When the men of the family grew up and married, they would each establish themselves near or far, while the old people and the girls remained in the original house till all the children were married or the parents died, or, more commonly, brought up children to inherit the usufruct of the land and occupy the house.'[1]

Certain points which appear in this description are confirmed by other sources. There was a definite preference for matrilocal marriage. Even when the newly wed couple were not to remain permanently in the house of the bride's parents, convention required them to remain for a period of days or weeks after the wedding before moving elsewhere. Wilkinson[2] points out however that the average Malay peasant's house was not large enough to contain the original husband and wife and a married daughter with her husband and children. When the grandchildren arrived, the younger couple had either to build a house of their own nearby (hence the homestead 'cluster' configuration) or enlarge the old house. Matrilocal marriage where it occurred is thus to be understood in terms of residence in the same homestead rather than the same house as the bride's parents. In the same passage Wilkinson[2] admits that matrilocal marriage was a norm of convention and that economic factors (scarcity of land or the husband's interests further away) often compelled the married couple to establish themselves at a distance from the homestead of the bride's parents.

The sons left the homestead of their parents when they married and settled with their wives' families or elsewhere. In time therefore the homestead came to consist of sisters (or women more remotely related in the female line) together with their husbands and children.

The homestead group was exogamous but this rule was expressed in terms of rules against incest with kindred and not in terms of group exogamy. In general there was no marriage with kinsfolk nearer than second cousins. By contrast the village was not an exogamous unit.[3] On the contrary intermarriage between groups in the same village was common. A man who married out of his village took for his wife a woman who was a foreigner as well as a stranger, unless he found her in a village culturally akin to his own. This was a considerable inducement to him to marry within his own village. If he was a member of a family of high status in the village, he would also prefer to remain in the circle where his position was recognized. But village endogamy, although it was quite usual, was

---

[1] Swettenham (1948), p. 136.   [2] Wilkinson (1908a), p. 26.

[3] In the passage quoted above Swettenham refers to the sons establishing themselves as married men 'near or far' from their family home.

not a universal or an explicitly preferred practice in the norms of village life.

To sum up, the village community consisted of one or more groups of kinsfolk whose identity as groups was often marked by residence in separate homesteads (and also by co-operation in working the fields and other economic activity). In the first generation each group of kinsfolk consisted of the founder of the group, his wife and children, and possibly also of his brothers, sisters and the various spouses and children of those relatives. In later generations the group of kinsfolk consisted of sisters (or women more remotely related in the matrilineal line), their husbands (who might be by birth members of the same village community) and their children. It might also happen that a son or other patrilineal descendant of the founder of the group remained as the head of the group of his sisters, etc. (a patrilocal marriage in this case). The different groups in the village were linked by intermarriage.

AUTHORITY IN THE VILLAGE

In a village which was the residence of a chief, the chief himself or more commonly one of his sons or brothers acted as village headman. In villages where there was no chief, the headman might still be an aristocratic connexion of the chief of the district. But more often the headman of a village (called *penghulu*) was a member of one of the village family groups and was not of the aristocratic class.

Swettenham describes the position as follows:

'In every village in Perak there is or ought to be a headman—the *Penghulu*. This office he has probably inherited (at least he looks upon it as partly an inheritance) from his father or other near relation. The sympathies of the villagers are with him, he is personally known to all, related to many, his influence is greater or smaller in proportion to the number or fewness of his relations or following, the character he bears, the years he has been in office, the position he holds in the esteem of his *Raja* and the amount of his private property.'[1]

Other sources state that a headman was 'related to half his mukim',[2] and that he was invariably chosen from among the principal landowners of the village.[3]

In these descriptions the following qualifications can be distinguished. (1) The headman often inherited his office from his father or other patrilineal relative; (2) he was a member of a numerous and prominent family group in the village; (3) he was related to a considerable number of his fellow villagers; (4) he was relatively wealthy; (5) he had the support of his superior in the political hierarchy; and (6) he had prestige arising from his personal abilities. These points are discussed briefly in the following paragraphs.

[1] *SSD*, 28 May 1883.   [2] Winstedt, quoted in *AR Pk*, 1909.

[3] McNair, *SSD*, 28 May 1883.

(1) *Patrilineal descent.* There are several recorded instances of a son succeeding his father which bear out the proposition that the office of headman was to some extent inherited in that line. But there were exceptions; a son did not automatically succeed his father—he merely had a good claim to do so.

The factor of patrilineal descent in the choice of a headman makes an interesting contrast with the preference for matrilocal marriage and the custom under which houses and land generally passed from mother to daughter. It follows that a son of a headman had to marry within his own village, or, if he married outside, must bring his wife to live in patrilocal marriage in his village, in order to retain the prestige of being a son of a village headman and in order to be able to assert a claim to succeed to the office of headman when his father died.

(2) *Leading family.* The family of the founder of the village had the best claim to provide the headman in later generations—both by the patrilineal descent rule and by general prestige. But as a village grew older other families came to the fore by reason of wealth, aristocratic patronage. the personal ability or the Islamic prestige of individuals among them, In these circumstances the 'founder family' could lose its monopoly of the office of headman. In Perak in 1875 there were many villages with no acknowledged headman. In some the office was vacant, in others the office was disputed between claimants appointed by different superior authorities.[1] This situation was in part a result of the fact that between 1871 and 1874 there had been two claimants to the Sultanate of Perak, each canvassing popular support. It is at least clear that in many villages more than one group of kinsmen could lay claim to the office of headman.

(3) and (4) *Kinship Ties* and *Wealth.* The importance of these factors needs no explanation. The headman had no force at his back to induce obedience to his orders. His authority, although political in its function, rested on non-political bases.

(5) *Support of Higher Authority.* The support of higher political authority was in form a coercive element (from the point of view of the village) in the authority of the headman. The formal power of appointment of a headman rested with the Sultan and was expressed in a letter of authority (*surat kuasa*) under the Sultan's seal. In practice the power of the Sultan in the 1870's was so weak that the appointment of a village headman was usually made by a district chief only. The headman either had no letter of authority at all or only a letter from his district chief instead of his Sultan.

Moreover the nominal backing of higher authority was not effective as a coercive sanction of authority. A district chief was unable to impose a headman who lacked local support in his village unless the chief was willing to back his nominee by force—a most uneconomical use of the chief's

[1] *SSD*, 26 April 1875.

limited military resources. The chief therefore sounded village opinion before deciding which candidate to support by his official recognition. In some cases the chief even conducted an election to determine who should be headman (heads of homesteads acted as electors).[1] In such elections one may perhaps detect the influence of Menangkabau custom which was the cultural heritage but not the basis of political authority in many villages in Perak.

In choosing a headman the district chief was concerned to appoint a headman who would be loyal to himself and who would administer the village satisfactorily. It is thus convenient to pass on from the appointment of village headmen to their functions.

A headman, although chosen as the leader of a community, was in form responsible for an area of territory and incidentally for the people in it. In practice this distinction was not important. The headman's authority was confined to his village as the only inhabited part of his territory. The empty jungle did not matter.[2]

The headman was responsible for keeping the peace—more by conciliation than by coercion; for arresting criminals and delivering them to the district chief for trial; for providing labour from the village under the corvée (kerah) system; for raising a defence levy when required; and for executing the various other requirements of the district chief.

The headman was merely the most senior of a group of village leaders, rather than a sole autocrat. In his work he was assisted by the Mata-Mata —a deputy, village constable and sergeant at arms.[3] More important in the hierarchy of village authority was the Imam (vicar) of the mosque. Every village of any size had a mosque which was its only public building and an object of much local pride. The Friday prayer meeting made the mosque a forum for discussion of village affairs (after the prayers were over). The Imam was usually drawn from one of the leading families of the village. In the political history of the 1870's in Perak Imams appear as 'principal men' in their villages and often played a political role as confidants and advisers to the village headmen. The Imam was not necessarily a man of great Islamic learning but he had often made the pilgrimage to Mecca. Although the Imam was usually a member of a leading family in the village, it was probably easier for a villager not born to high status to achieve it as Imam than as village headman (an office more strictly reserved for one of the village notables). An Imam was addressed by the honorific prefix Tuan (Sir).

[1] SSD, 28 May 1883, records that a headman of Sungei Terap (in the Kinta District of Perak) had been elected 'by heads of households in conformity with ancient custom'.

[2] In modern times the Penghulu is responsible for a mukim, a sub-district which may include several villages; the headman of a single village is called ketua kampong (or in some areas penggawa and sidang). Mukim denotes the area served by a mosque and is sometimes translated 'parish'.

[3] Literally Mata-Mata means 'the eyes'. In modern times it denotes a policeman.

In addition to the *Imam* there were lesser officers of the mosque such as the *Bilal* (Caller to Prayer) and the *Khatib* (Reciter). Moreover every head of a homestead ranked as an elder (*ketua*). The elders (*ketua-tuaan*) took part in the discussion of village affairs and negotiated the settlement of quarrels and disputes between their respective groups. Finally the village had its magician (*pawang*) who led the fertility rituals and doctored the sick.

VILLAGES IN NEGRI SEMBILAN

The situation in Negri Sembilan differed from that in Perak and Selangor by reason of the greater predominance of Menangkabau influence in Negri Sembilan and its recognition as a basis for political organization.

There is a danger of exaggerating these differences by setting up clear-cut stereotypes of Negri Sembilan social structure (the *'adat perpateh*) and the social structure of the other Peninsular States (the *'adat temenggong*). Wilkinson commenting on the two systems of 'law' connected with this distinction said that the differences were 'superficial and are connected with the way the law is administered rather than in the actual law itself'; the *'adat temenggong* was 'the *'adat perpateh* administered on autocratic lines'.[1] Wilkinson's phrase 'administered on autocratic lines' hints at what would appear to be the vital distinction between the situation in Negri Sembilan and elsewhere. The Malay communities of Perak and Selangor had grown up for centuries under a political regime derived from the model of the Malacca Sultanate and from the Hindu kingdoms of a still earlier period. Menangkabau influence existed in Perak as in Negri Sembilan (though admittedly it was less pervasive in Perak). This influence however had in Perak (unlike Negri Sembilan) always been subordinated to and denied political recognition by a regime of Sultan and chiefs who were themselves organized in patrilineal descent groups and whose authority was exercised on a territorial basis (in contrast to the clan/lineage political system of Negri Sembilan). In Perak, and also in Selangor, the peasant class were thus administered in villages and districts as territorial units. If they had been minded to organize themselves in clans, they would not have been allowed to do so. Kinship ties had no significance outside the small world of village life.

It can be argued that the situation in Perak and Selangor was merely the result of cultural heterogeneity. In those states the Menangkabau element was not predominant enough; the lack of any dominant social system precluded the possibility of a political system based (as it was in Negri Sembilan) on a social system. A centralized autocracy was inevitable

[1] Wilkinson (1908b). De Jong (1951) argues that *'adat perpateh* and *'adat temenggong* might be anglicisms and not Malay concepts at all. *'Adat perpateh* seems to be an indigenous expression.

as a means of holding culturally diverse elements together.[1] If this argument be accepted, the failure of Menangkabau culture to gain political recognition in Perak and Selangor was merely the result of its own comparative weakness in relation to other cultures represented among the subject class of those States. It is probable however that the time factor, mentioned in the preceding paragraph, also played its part. In Perak, and to a lesser extent in Selangor, there was an established ruling class with its institutions such as the Sultanate before there was any considerable number of Menangkabau settlers. In Negri Sembilan the order was reversed.

Negri Sembilan had no Sultanate or other organ of central government until about 1780. At the time of the Malacca Sultans (c. 1400–1511 A.D.) a small ruling class dependent on Malacca had been established. But these rulers were no more than local district headmen. In the 250 years between the fall of the Malacca Sultanate and the establishment of a royal dynasty in Negri Sembilan there was a large flow of immigration mainly but not entirely from Menangkabau.

These immigrants, who came in small groups, brought with them the vestiges of a system of alignment into lineages based on matrilineal descent. One must say 'the vestiges of a system' because the circumstances of migration in small groups made it impossible for them to bring with them the actuality of kinship ties extending beyond small groups. They did however bring the idea of such a system and, as will be explained, rebuild their social order upon it.

The small number of Malacca chiefs already established in Negri Sembilan came to terms with the immigrants. The Malacca families were accepted as the ruling class and the titular owners of the soil. In each district of Negri Sembilan[2] there was thus one group acknowledged as the 'heirs of the country' (*waris negri*) entitled to provide the ruling chief of the district. These *waris* groups, originally patrilineal after the tradition of the Malacca Sultanate, intermarried with the matrilineal Menangkabau immigrants and in time assimilated their own rules for transmission of political office to the matrilineal model. In most cases this change had occurred long before the nineteenth century but in Sungei Ujong, a major district of Negri Sembilan in which matrilineal influence was weaker than elsewhere, the change from patrilineal to matrilineal transmission of the district chieftainship occurred as late as 1800 A.D. In that case the change was due to a succession dispute within the *waris* group in which a uterine nephew of a former chief found that it suited him to assert that the succession ought to be on a matrilineal basis.[3] It may be supposed that in other districts internal divisions among the *waris* facilitated the absorption of the culture of their subjects.

[1] See passage from Fortes and Evans-Pritchard (1940) quoted at p. 26 above.
[2] The name *Negri Sembilan* (Nine Districts) is no older than 1800.
[3] Wilkinson (1911), p. 31: a fuller account at p. 78 below.

By way of digression it is interesting to note how myth was used to ease the transition to matriliny among the *waris*. As an historical fact[1] the *waris* derived their primacy from the appointment of their patrilineal forbears to be chiefs by the Bendaharas (Chief Ministers) of the Malacca Sultanate. In all other 'succession States' it was sufficient thus to derive title from the Malacca Sultanate. But in Negri Sembilan the heirs of Malacca had changed over to matrilineal succession to political office. It was necessary therefore to find a matrilineal title to justify their position. This was achieved by claiming that the founders of their families were the sons of Sakai (aborigine) ancestresses married to Malacca noblemen. Certain of the *waris* groups even called themselves *Biduanda*, a word used in some contexts to mean Sakai. In this way they were able to argue that by aborigine ancestry on the maternal side they were entitled to primacy over mere matrilineal immigrants.[2]

The *waris negri*, thus organized on matrilineal lines, provided the chief of each district. The four major district chiefs of Negri Sembilan were known as *Undang* ('Lawgiver'—more or less). Until 1780 these chiefs formed a loose confederacy for defence purposes. Apart from that confederacy there was no other structure of central political organization.

Perhaps because of the lack of a central organ and symbol around which the *waris* groups could gather in distinction from the immigrants, there was no important social contrast of status between the *waris* and the first arrivals among the Menangkabau immigrants. They were conscious of being different—the Malacca families were *waris* and the immigrants were *suku*—but there was no sentiment of super- and sub-ordination in the distinction. This lack of a formal class structure with a division between chiefs' families as a ruling class and immigrants as a subject class was a phenomenon of some importance. There was no barrier to the emergence of a political system based on the descent grouping of the immigrants.

The immigrants accepted the political primacy of the *waris* only on limited terms. The district chief (*Undang*) was drawn from the *waris* but the choice of the individual to fill the office rested with the leaders of the immigrants as electors.[3] Moreover a district chief was not allowed to interfere between the leaders of the immigrant groups and their own people.

[1] e.g. see Winstedt (1934b), p. 43.

[2] Winstedt (op. cit.,) discusses this myth. See also Winstedt (1932), pp. 135–42 'Bendahara Sekudai and Negri Sembilan', and Gullick (1949), pp. 7–13. The fact that Bendahara Sekudai, mythical progenitor of the *waris*, was an historical figure who visited Negri Sembilan about 1644 enables us to date the approximate period of the myth. On the complex meaning of *Biduanda* see Wilkinson (1932).

[3] The details of these elective arrangements differed from one district to another. It is a fair generalization to say that the *waris* chose a candidate (subject to their own rules of rotation between sub-groups in the *waris*) and the immigrant leaders had the right to confirm or reject him. Rejection meant civil war.

The first-comers among the immigrants purchased (*tebus*) considerable tracts of unoccupied land from the *waris*. This purchase consisted in the transfer of conventional gifts as an acknowledgement of their title rather than a payment of economic value. Land was abundant and had no value.[1] The land thus purchased (*tanah tebus*), whether occupied (*tanah hidup*—land alive) or unoccupied (*tanah mati*—land dead), was controlled by the purchasers and their matrilineal descendants. This situation underlay the claim of the first-comers to primacy over later immigrants.

As has been said, the immigrants brought with them the concept of social organization into large groups and smaller sub-groups based on matrilineal descent. In Negri Sembilan they organized themselves into a similar if slightly artificial system. Groups of immigrants who were actually related by common descent became *perut* (the word means 'womb' and denotes descent from a common ancestress—it will hereafter be translated 'lineage'). An original lineage was often a local village settlement group. Lineages settled in the same district which were conscious of the bond of common clan membership in Menangkabau grouped themselves into district clans (*suku*).[2] These groupings were strictly limited to one district. Lineages of similar origin settled in two different districts recognized no bond of association.

Each lineage had a headman (*ibu bapa*—parent). Each clan (*suku*) had a clan headman (*lembaga*).[3] The clan headman was chosen by the lineage headmen subject to a rule that the office must be held in turn (*giliran*) by a man from each lineage in the clan. The clan headmen as a group represented the immigrants in their dealings with the district chief; this fact was often formalized by constituting a chief's council of which the clan headmen were members.

The *waris* assimilated themselves to this model. The *waris* group of each district was equated with a clan (but it was always called *waris* never *suku*) and it was divided into matrilineages each with their headmen. The office of district chief was filled by rotation among the lineages of the *waris* clan.

The system so far described relates to the earliest phase of political development in Negri Sembilan during the seventeenth and eighteenth centuries. Immigration went on and not all the later arrivals were Menangkabau men. The descendants of the first immigrants were thus confronted with a problem of absorption. They solved the problem in one of two ways. Individuals or small family groups could be adopted (*kadimkan*) into existing lineages, especially if it was felt to be necessary

---

[1] See above, p. 28, n. 5.

[2] The word *suku* means 'quarter' or 'section'. There was a marked preference for organization on a basis of four units.

[3] The word *lembaga* means 'origin' or 'ancient custom'. Its use as a title of office is a special usage of Negri Sembilan.

to gain numbers. But the large flow of immigration and the non-Menangkabau status of some of the newcomers induced a certain reluctance among the descendants of the first immigrants to dilute the privileges of 'early settler' standing by admitting all and sundry to equality with themselves. The alternative to individual adoption was the absorption of later immigrants as separate *groups*, either lineages or clans, of inferior status.

It thus happened that when a band of later immigrants asked to be allowed to take up unused land within the territory (*tanah tebus*) of an established clan or lineage, they were admitted to the 'circle' (*limbongan*) of the earlier settlers but not to their privileges. They were given land and accepted as a recognized group. But, if admitted to a clan as a lineage, they did not have the right to provide a clan headman in turn with the older lineages. If admitted as a separate clan, they did not send their clan headman to sit in the council of the district chief; they remained as a 'client clan' of the clan in whose territory they had settled.

Clan headmen of immigrant groups were set in authority over people (the members of their clan) not all of whom lived in a contiguous block of territory. The district chiefs were territorial rulers with authority over everyone within their districts but this was subject to the proviso that clan headmen stood between the district chief and the commoner member of the clan. A district chief who had cause for complaint against an individual was expected to send for the clan headman who was responsible for the individual as his clansman. An individual who wanted the help of higher authority went first to his lineage headman; the latter referred the matter to the clan headman; he in turn took the matter to the district chief. There was an elaborate code of matters within the jurisdiction of each dignitary. It appears that in practice a district chief who was strong enough disregarded the niceties of this code. But such conduct was irregular by the acknowledged standards of Negri Sembilan custom.

The system described above is set out diagrammatically on page 42.

In contrast to the Perak/Selangor situation there was no clear-cut dividing line of class distinction between the district chief's family (the *waris*) and the long-settled immigrants. In particular they intermarried freely. The distinction between long-settled immigrants and late-comers was a matter of tacit behaviour rather than of explicit status. It was marked in a reluctance on the part of the privileged groups to intermarry with the newcomers and in the denial of equality of rights to political office for them.

This description of the Negri Sembilan situation has passed from a discussion of village life to a preliminary consideration of the higher political organization. This is unavoidable since in Negri Sembilan the two subjects were closely related. It is impossible to explain why there was no village headman in Negri Sembilan without first describing how

D

the villager was integrated for political purposes into a system of large kinship groups.

To pass on to the subject of village leadership in Negri Sembilan: the composition of village populations in Negri Sembilan was not unlike the situation in the other states. Each of the long-settled lineages had an original focus of settlement and very often took its name from it. For example, in the Rembau district each of the subdivisions of the *waris* group is known as *Kampong* Kota, etc. In time however the members of

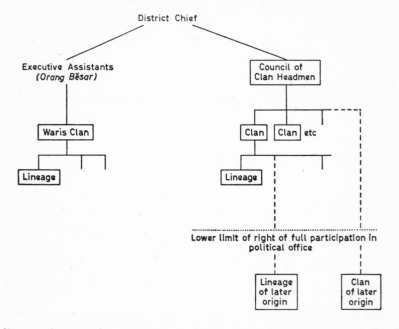

lineages became dispersed over more than one village and each village came to include more than the members of one lineage only.[1] Clans never had been compact units of territorial settlement.

The sentiment of kinship grouping on a larger scale than the village was strong enough to prevent the emergence of a system of territorial village headmen. Members of a minority group in a village looked to their lineage headman, even if he were some distance away, as their leader. Within each village the senior member of the leading lineage was the leader of his own group and, to a lesser extent, of the village community. Matrilocal marriage must have affected the situation since it would tend to take the adult males of each lineage away from the group unless they had married women of other lineages in the same village.

[1] *AR NS*, 1893. 'Members of one tribe being scattered about in different portions of a District or State.'

POLITICAL ASPECTS OF MALAY VILLAGE LIFE

A political system must be adapted to the society which it controls. It is a part of the social system to which it contributes order and stability. There are certain elements in the village life described in this section which explain why the political system, to be described in later sections, was as it was.

A variety of factors induced the Malay peasants to settle in village communities along the banks of rivers. The needs of economic and other co-operation in living together obliged these villages to evolve their own leadership in the form of village headmen. Here was the basic group formation upon which the political system was built up, viz. people grouped in village communities with their own leaders and sited along river communications which they needed as an essential part of their economy.

Except in Negri Sembilan the village population had no basis of association in groups larger than villages. In terms of descent, kinship and culture they were so heterogeneous and discrete as to have no natural alignment into larger groups. The need for widespread order and stability which the village could not provide was met by the imposition of an external control of district chiefs and rulers of States.

This higher political system served especially to meet the social need for organization of defence, trade and law. If the villages had lived in anarchy with each other these needs would not have been met satisfactorily. Trade could not have moved up and down rivers without some sort of 'King's Peace' along the length of the rivers. Trade in turn provided the revenue by which the rulers siphoned off resources for the maintenance of the system which they embodied.

Malay settlement was transitory and impermanent. There was much migration and local movement. This fact provided a mechanism by which the subjects exercised control over their rulers. Flight was the final sanction against bad government. There was a second aspect of this instability which deserves mention. It had the inevitable result that many individuals found themselves separated by the accidents of migration and war from their kindred. So far as they could, they got themselves re-absorbed into a village community. But outsiders of a different cultural group were not welcome in a village to which they did not belong. In the social need to anchor this flotsam and jetsam is to be found the making of the chief's 'followers' and 'debt-slaves' to be mentioned hereafter. The need, as so often, was reciprocal. The homeless fighting man needed a patron. The chief on the other hand needed a private army as the basis of his authority.

3

The Sultanate

THE ROLE OF THE SULTAN

The apex of the political system of each State was the ruler called *Yang di-Pertuan* (He who is made lord), *Raja* (Hindu Ruler) and *Sultan* (Arabic Ruler). Whatever may have been the case in earlier periods, the Sultan (as he will hereafter be called[1]) did not in most States of the nineteenth century embody any exceptional concentration of administrative authority. Powerful district chiefs could and sometimes did flout his wishes with impunity; some of them were wealthier than he was. A Sultan was generally in control of a royal district which he governed after the fashion of a district chief. But his role in the political system of the State, as distinct from his additional and local role of district chief of the royal district, did not consist in the exercise of pre-eminent power.

The Sultan's role was to symbolize and to some extent to preserve the unity of the State. In the Malay States there were many forces tending towards conflict and disintegration. Except in Negri Sembilan there was a lack of cultural homogeneity in the subject class. In all States the existence of district chiefs constituted foci of purely local power and influence. It is true of course that the opposition of the chiefs to each other tended to neutralize their disruptive potentialities in regard to central authority. The chiefs however were often at odds with the Sultan as much as with each other. They certainly resisted the exercise of any royal authority in their districts. Yet the hard facts of trade, national defence and the need for law and order over a wider area than a district dictated the preservation of peace if the State was not to disintegrate completely. (Civil wars were indeed of frequent occurrence.)

Hence there was an acceptance of the Sultanate, if not of the Sultan, as the formal head of the State. Chiefs fought and intrigued to put one claimant on the throne instead of another but never to destroy the Sultanate itself. Government was *kerajaan*, the state of having a ruler, and they visualized no other system.

It commonly happens that symbols of group unity are invested with

[1] The royal ruler of Negri Sembilan was not called *Sultan* but only *Yang di-Pertuan Besar* (colloquially abbreviated to *Yam Tuan*). This distinction was correlated with his limited powers as a mere paramount and the fact that his title did not derive from Malacca.

an aura of sanctity and supernatural power. The Sultan of a State was vested with majesty (*daulat*) at his installation. He then became different from himself as he had been before and from his royal kinsmen. It was believed that any Malay who infringed the majesty of the Sultan would suffer retribution from the impersonal force of outraged royal dignity.[1]

The many expressions of this concept of royal majesty as a supernatural power were derived from origins of Indonesian, Muslim Indian, and Hindu ritual and belief.[2] The adoption of these elements in the political system of the nineteenth century Malay States is of course to be interpreted in terms of social function in the situation of that period. The ancient origins explain the source not the need for such ideas.

The person of the Sultan was sacred and any touching of it was forbidden. It was said that white blood ran in his veins. There was no evidence that this attribute was seriously believed in. It was part of the conventional make-believe used to express the sense of royal dignity. The use of symbols seems to beget a need for elaboration beyond what common experience of the community knows to be true in order that the attitude to the symbols may find adequate expression. Some of the curious aspects of totemism can perhaps be explained in this way.

At ceremonies the Sultan sat impassive; immobility was a sign of divinity. Yellow clothing (and hangings, state umbrellas, etc.) was a royal monopoly. The installation of a Sultan was marked by the most elaborate ritual, including a ceremonial washing to mark the making of a new man.

The sacredness of a Sultan's person was communicated to his regalia (*kebesaran*—symbols of greatness). The details of the royal regalia differed in different States but the general composition was the same. They included:

(1) Musical instruments such as royal drums (*gendang nobat*), pipes, flutes and trumpets. The royal musicians were commoners but enjoyed high status. The instruments were not much used.

(2) Various insignia of office such as sceptre (*kayu gamit*), betel box (*puan naga taru*), jewel (*kamala*), a spoken secret formula (*surat chiri*), a seal of state (*chap halilintar*) and umbrella (*ubar-ubar*), pillows, hangings, &c. These were used or displayed on ritual occasions.

(3) Weapons such as swords, lances and the long dagger of execution (*keris panjang*).[3]

---

[1] The Malay expression is *timpa daulat*—to be struck down by majesty as by a thunderbolt. It is significant that it was believed that the supernatural power of royalty might be less effective against a Chinese because he was an outsider (see Skeat (1900), p. 41). Royal majesty and membership of the group over which the Sultan ruled were inter-related and co-extensive in operation.

[2] This topic is discussed at length in Winstedt (1947b) and Skeat, op. cit.

[3] Skeat (1900), pp. 25–7.

These objects were believed to be self-created and to be so filled with supernatural power as to blast any unauthorized person who handled them.

The royal drums, played only at the installation of a Sultan, were perhaps the most sacred of all the regalia. The yellow or white umbrella is or was a common royal insignia in many societies of South-East Asia. The inclusion of weapons in the regalia is partly to be explained by the power of life and death theoretically reserved to the Sultan alone and partly by his rarely exercised role as leader of defence forces in foreign wars. There was a considerable Malay preoccupation with weapons as symbols of military power[1]—a symbolism common enough in all societies.

There were many forms of clothing, weapons, domestic and household adornment reserved to the Sultan alone. There was a special vocabulary called the *bahasa dalam* (the language within [the palace]) used in referring to the movements and activities of the Sultan. The house in which he lived had a special title—*Istana* (Palace). It was vacated at his death and, resources permitting, a new one was built for his successor. After his death the Sultan was no longer known by the name he had born in his lifetime. Instead he was referred to as *Marhum* (*Almarhum*—the late Sultan) followed by some descriptive term, usually indicating the place of the Sultan's death or burial, e.g. *Marhum Tambelan* (the Sultan who died at Tambelan). It may be that the personal name was avoided for fear of involuntarily attracting the attention of the still potent spirit of the late ruler. In addressing a living Sultan it was customary to begin with a thousand pardons for thus troubling him.

Certain animals, fruits and even people were reserved to the Sultan. In different States this category included turtles' eggs, elephant tusks, the fruit of the *ketiar* tree, albino buffaloes and illegitimate children. Tame elephants were the mounts of royalty and it was thus appropriate that ivory should be royal property. Albino buffaloes were freaks and illegitimate children were members of society born contrary to its rules. There was thus an aura of abnormality and accursedness. A Sultan vested with supernatural power was the appropriate person to handle such beings.

There were comparatively few ceremonies in which a Sultan appeared as the leader of his people in temporal matters or in intercession with supernatural powers. His symbolic role was passive not active. The major public occasions of his reign were his installation and his funeral. The chiefs of the State took their customary part in the rituals of these occasions. There was a large gathering of the subject class but still only a fraction of the total population of the State. Communications did not permit the convocation of large assemblies of the common people. On the major festivals of the Muslim year, such as the end of the Fasting Month, the

---

[1] See below, p. 123.

Sultan held a levee at which some if not all his chiefs made obeisance (*menghadap*) to him.[1]

It was widely believed that the Sultan by his personal influence or good luck could bring or ward off pestilence and bad harvests. Swettenham writing of Perak in 1890 noted:

'. . . the other day the Sultan informed me that a succession of bad harvests . . . had been ascribed to the influence of the Resident and, he added politely, the Sultan'.[2]

The extension of the supernatural potency to an alien ruler (the Resident) indicates the association of supernatural potency with the position of being a ruler.

The elaborate apparatus of belief in the dignity and supernatural power of the Sultan needs to be contrasted with some actual behaviour of chiefs. The approved norm of conduct towards a Sultan was clear-cut; a chief must treat his ruler with deep respect. The tradition of Malay history contained moral tales to reinforce this attitude. For example, a *Bendahara* (Chief Minister) of the Malacca Sultanate submitted to an unjust sentence of death from his master, reproving his son who would have resisted with the remark 'It is the custom of the Malays that they shall never be disloyal to their Raja'.[3]

The formal submission of the chiefs to the Sultan was symbolized and expressed in the obeisance (*menghadap*) ceremony which merits a brief description. Obeisance had to be made by all chiefs at the installation of a Sultan, by an individual chief on first appointment to office and by the chiefs generally at intervals.[4] In each such ceremony the chiefs in turn

[1] There is an interesting indication of customary obligations of chiefs to make obeisance in the terms of the Negri Sembilan treaty of 1898. A generation before, the major district chiefs of Negri Sembilan had repudiated the titular paramountcy of the Yam Tuan over the State and had thereafter behaved as independent rulers of their districts (thereby reverting to the situation which had existed before a royal dynasty was established in the State about 1780). As a result of much patient diplomacy by the Yam Tuan and the British Resident the four major chiefs (the Undang) were persuaded in 1898 to acknowledge the Yam Tuan again as *primus inter pares* among themselves and paramount ruler of the whole State. This settlement was expressed in a written agreement to record the obligations and rights of the parties between themselves. It is a short agreement of only six brief clauses. The fifth clause records that the Undang shall not be obliged to attend at the royal court on the second day of feasting after the month of fasting but that they shall be present on major domestic occasions in the royal family such as a wedding or a circumcision. The inference is that if the position had not been thus explicitly defined, the Yam Tuan as royal ruler might have required the chiefs, *by custom*, to attend on the Muslim feast day. Formal attendance involves formal obeisance. On obeisance see below, p. 48.

[2] *AR Pk*, 1890. See also Skeat (1900), p. 36: 'He is firmly believed to possess a personal influence over the works of nature such as the growth of crops and the bearing of fruit trees.'

[3] C. C. Brown (1952), p. 163.

[4] See p. 139, n. 1, as to obeisance on Muslim feast days.

approached the dais on which the ruler sat. The chief began his approach by sitting down cross-legged on the ground some yards in front of the dais and facing it. He then drew his legs under him and to one side and thus advanced, putting forward his hands, palm downwards, on the ground in front of him and drawing his body forward to his hands. Between each forward move he raised his hands, with palms together, until his thumbs were level with his eyebrows and almost touched them—the exact height of the hands in this movement were one of the niceties of the movement. Having approached to the dais and put his hands between the hands of the Sultan, the chief withdrew backwards, still facing the dais, to his original starting position and then walked backwards to resume his correct position in the levee as a whole. It was a formal and public act of obeisance performed in the presence of a large concourse of people in the Sultan's hall of audience.[1]

There is evidence from modern times[2] that some chiefs at least brought themselves to this formal and public obeisance only with difficulty. At home in their districts they were magnates to whom their subjects abased themselves with only slightly less ceremony. They did not in fact submit to the government of the Sultan except to a very limited extent. Their obeisance was not therefore the mere acknowledgement of the facts of power but rather a contrast with them. Obeisance ceremonies were evidently occasions of tension. The Sultan of Selangor said in the 1870's of the period before British rule that he was never more in fear of assassination than at the obeisance ceremonies.[3]

Why then did the ceremonies of obeisance, sometimes unwelcome to both sides, take place at all? They had come to be the symbolic expression of the position of the Sultanate as the apex of a political system which the district chiefs wished to preserve. The Sultan was not reckoned to be the acknowledged ruler of the State *vis-à-vis* a particular chief unless the chief had made obeisance to him and continued to do so on appropriate occasions. The chiefs, except in Negri Sembilan, derived the title of their authority from the Sultan under the constitutional theory of the Malay

---

[1] This account is based on the writer's observations at two such ceremonies in Negri Sembilan in 1945 and 1946. There is no reason to think that the formalities changed in the previous seventy years.

[2] The writer, as an administrative officer, had to make the arrangements in 1945 for a newly appointed district chief of Jelebu (Negri Sembilan) to make obeisance to the Yam Tuan. A clan headman objected to the principle of a chief of Jelebu making obeisance in this way. He said that it had never happened in the past and that the newly appointed chief would be considered mad if he did so. In fact there had been a triennial obeisance ceremony in 1937 (the sequence was interrupted by the war); the clan headman had been in office at that time. The former district chief had undoubtedly made obeisance in 1937 and it would have been a breach of custom if the same clan headman among others had not been in attendance on his chief at the time.

[3] Innes (1885).

State. They could not claim to hold office unless they had been appointed by the Sultan, which incidentally imported the necessity of obeisance to him. A chief's power was derivative and in controversial or important acts he sought the Sultan's approval. Thus the chiefs who planned the assassination of the first British Resident of Perak in 1875 obtained a letter of authority from the Sultan and also money and munitions—the latter a symbol of approval as well as material aid. In the Selangor civil war both sides appealed to the Sultan from time to time and 'His Highness was always requested to give tangible proof of his approval in the shape of gunpowder and lead'.[1]

There was a contradiction in the relation between Sultans and chiefs. The chiefs, in whom most of the real power was vested, were obliged by the threat of external attack, the need for a larger trade unit than the inland district and by the sheer facts of geography to preserve the State as a unit. The Sultanate was the symbol of State unity. It was also, like medieval kingship, the fount of nobility and the source of all aristocratic titles. There was thus an ambivalence of attitude; the chiefs showed formal respect and sought formal approval from the Sultan as the basis of their own position. Yet they were reluctant to submit to the Sultan by obeisance because they lost dignity thereby. The strict ceremonial of the obeisance can be regarded as a sort of mechanism of Aristotelian *katharsis*. The chief had to steel himself to make obeisance. Afterwards there was a certain temporary relief to have got it over which eased the friction inherent in the structural relationship of Sultan and chief.

Since the Sultan had so little real power of government he had no need of an elaborate machine of central government. The Malacca tradition provided titles of high offices of a central government.[2] These titles had been preserved but were appropriated by district chiefs who did not perform the functions associated with the offices which they held. The Sultan had a circle of confidants and advisers but these were not usually important chiefs.[3]

The Sultan was the undisputed agent of the community in the field of external affairs and defence. As the embodiment of the unity of the State he was responsible for its preservation in contacts with external forces. Between 1830 and 1870 however there were no serious foreign wars or threats of war. The *pax Britannica* was extended to the Malay States by the mere existence of force in the Straits Settlements. The Sultan's functions as a leader in war thus dwindled away in inactivity. The civil

---

[1] Swettenham (1895), p. 104.

[2] See above, p. 8 for a list of these offices.

[3] On the circle of advisers see below, p. 51. On the incongruity of title and function see Swettenham (1948), p. 120: 'In Perak there has survived the most perfect organization of State officers, each with well-defined duties; only, in 1872, the duties were ignored and the titles were simply used as a cover for the exercise of a large authority.'

wars of 1865–1875 were more between chiefs than against the Sultan. In Pahang however a chief rose in rebellion and the Sultan mobilized chiefs to suppress him. Where a Sultan did act to preserve peace and unity, he could do so only by mobilizing the forces of those chiefs who would accept his leadership.

In foreign affairs the Sultan was more active than in war. In this field also he acted as the leader of a coalition of chiefs. It was recognized that no commitment in the external sphere, such as making a treaty with a foreign power, was valid and binding on the chiefs unless they had joined in it. A treaty required the signature not only of the Sultan but also of a dozen or more leading chiefs. The exigencies of foreign policy brought the chiefs together in conclave with the Sultan more than anything else could do. The growing tension with the British in Perak in 1875 occasioned several of these meetings. The seating arrangements of one meeting are known and are of some interest:[1]

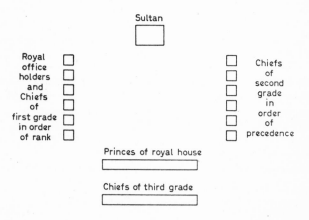

The most senior members of the council sat on the Sultan's right. The Malay words for 'right' and 'left' are also used to denote 'senior' and 'junior' respectively. Distance from the Sultan within each of the two senior groups was correlated with decreasing seniority. Position in relation to the Sultan was the means by which each aristocrat demonstrated his status relative to the rest of the gathering. It was a concrete instance of a general principle of Malay aristocratic life.

The meeting took place on the verandah or front room of the house, which was the customary scene of business activity (predominantly masculine) as distinct from the domestic activity (predominantly feminine) in the interior of a Malay house of any size and degree. Chiefs who were unable to be present in person at the meeting sent deputies with written

[1] The meeting took place on 21 July 1875. Particulars from *PCE*.

authority under seal to commit their principals. The importance of documents in Malay political life, not least in the field of agency, is mentioned later.[1]

In general chiefs who were neither present nor represented at a council were free to repudiate any decisions taken in their absence. If the absentee was unimportant compared with those who were present, the incompleteness of the conclave did not matter. But to stay away was the only mode of expressing disagreement available to a powerful chief. Etiquette did not permit him to differ publicly from his Sultan if the latter chose to express a definite opinion.[2] British administrators in Perak in 1875 spent much effort in trying to obtain the signatures of Perak chiefs who had not been present at Pangkor in 1874 to sign the Anglo-Malay treaty.

Convention required a Sultan to consult certain counsellors on all acts of state. These were (1) male members of the royal family close in the line of succession (the *waris negri*) and (2) chiefs of the first grade, conventionally four in number, and sometimes of the second grade (eight in number).[3] In practice the Sultan saw little of his major chiefs and was often at loggerheads with his close kinsmen. Contacts with chiefs were limited to councils to discuss foreign relations and ceremonial occasions such as installations, Muslim feast days and major domestic occasions such as a marriage. For the rest many chiefs were too powerful and too hostile to be willing to conform frequently to the submission to royalty required by court etiquette. In the opposite and less usual situation of a strong Sultan (such as happened in Pahang) the chiefs were too much afraid of the Sultan to come near him. Moreover in most cases a chief's district was so distant from the capital that to attend at court was to neglect more serious matters of district government.

THE SULTAN'S ADVISERS

For the day to day business of government the Sultan consulted an informal group of advisers. The constitution of this group varied in particular cases. A British administrator noted that in 1874 the Sultan of Perak's intimates were four chiefs, only one of the first grade, and three royal kinsmen, all young men who held no office. He commented that 'at times these chiefs exercise some influence over him but at others none'.[4] The Sultan of Pahang relied entirely on four advisers. One was an upstart

[1] See below, pp. 52-3.

[2] Wilkinson (1908a) relates what embarrassment could be caused by a British Resident who tried to elicit the opinions of Malay chiefs in the presence of their Sultan before the latter had expressed his view. The writer has known Malay chiefs in modern times ask for a private interview with a British Adviser because they felt unable to differ from their ruler in his presence.

[3] *SSD*, 15 October 1887. [4] *SSD*, 26 April 1875.

promoted to chieftainship by the Sultan; the second was a Tamil Indian who acted as treasurer and tax-collector; a third was a Malay secretary and man of affairs who had been born in another State; the fourth was a Pahang Malay who had spent some time in the Straits Settlements and who posed as an expert on 'European affairs'.[1]

The different composition of these two groups is to be explained in the different circumstances of the two Sultans. Sultan Abdullah of Perak owed his position to the chiefs who surrounded him. The Sultan of Pahang was strong enough to overawe his chiefs and to govern with the aid of men who owed their position to him. In both cases the Sultan had cut himself off from the general body of chiefs and royal kinsmen and relied on men to whom he was linked by a tie of dependence on one side or the other.

These confidants were men of aristocratic or of pseudo-aristocratic status. The Sultan's decisions, taken with the advice of his intimates, had then to be translated into action. For this purpose he made use of assistants of lower status as secretaries. It is here convenient to mention the use of written documents in the Malay political system.

Writing, both as literature and for communication, had been in use for several centuries. It enjoyed great prestige. At the fifteenth century court of the Sultans of Malacca a letter from a foreign ruler was carried through the town by an envoy mounted on an elephant. It was then read aloud to the Sultan in the presence of his court.[2] As another example a district chief in Perak in the 1870's called a meeting of his subjects in order that a letter from the Sultan might be read aloud publicly. A chief who sent a plenipotentiary representative on a mission would give him one or more blank sheets of paper each bearing the chief's seal. The representative could write on these sheets to give an undertaking binding on the chief. The practice was so common that it was a reasonable question to an emissary to ask whether he had such blank sealed papers as a measure of his powers to negotiate.

The impress of a seal was essential to give a document validity. The seal of office of a Sultan or a district chief was thus an important possession. In one case a Sultan gave as his pretext for postponing action the fact that his seal was broken and under repair. Only one craftsman in Perak was allowed to make or repair the royal seal. In another case the use of the Sultan's signet ring instead of his state seal on a document made its genuineness suspect.[3]

The use of written documents was confined to major acts of state. Its use was to provide evidence of an important decision; not of the exchange

[1] *SSD*, 15 October 1887.

[2] e.g. Brown (1952), p. 70: 'ordered that the letter should be fetched with due ceremony from the ship and borne in procession.'

[3] Gullick (1953a), p. 101.

of opinion leading up to it. Writing was used to record the agreement of chiefs to elect a Sultan, the appointment of a district chief or of a village headman, the grant of a territory and the terms of a treaty. It was also less often used to preserve accounts and for private memoranda.

Sultans and other aristocrats did not write the documents on which their seals were affixed. It is one of the paradoxes of the situation that many members of a ruling class which accorded importance to documents in political affairs were themselves illiterate. It is evident however that literacy was spreading by 1870. The older men, including at least two Sultans of the period, were still illiterate. There were no schools; reading and writing were taught by tutors employed in the houses of great men. It is likely that some at least of these tutors were wandering schoolmasters originally trained in the educational system of the Straits Settlements.

Even if a Sultan was literate, there were reasons why he should not write his own letters. The writing of letters was an exercise in calligraphy and composition. A letter badly written, torn or deficient in the elaborate courtesies of Malay epistolary style was an insult to the person to whom it was addressed.[1] Writing was thus a task for professionals. Aristocrats therefore employed secretaries who were generally commoners. These secretaries enjoyed some prestige by the standards of their class. The word *Kerani* (Clerk) was used as an honorific prefix to a personal name. But writing was no task for an aristocrat because aristocrats even if literate did not do it.

The secretaries in the households of Sultans and great chiefs were men of varied status and qualifications. The majority were commoners but a few had aristocratic connections. Many were returned pilgrims from Mecca with the prestige and knowledge of the world which attached to them from that fact.[2] Some were merely 'writers' and persons of no consequence. Others, as so often happens in a confidential relationship of personal service, acquired much influence with their masters. Thus it was said that the Sultan of Pahang could not be approached except through his secretary, Tuan Hitam, and that the secretary often went so far as to misread letters to his master.[3]

Secretaries, even the humbler ones, had to know of matters of secrecy and great importance. They were expected to show the utmost discretion. Sultan Abdullah of Perak had one of his clerks killed on the mere suspicion that he had given information to a British official in 1875.[4]

[1] Munshi Abdullah who was at one time a secretary in the entourage of Stamford Raffles relates how Raffles was quick to detect the studied insult of a letter sent to him with a corner torn. (*Hikayat Abdullah*.)

[2] A returned pilgrim was called a *Haji* and he was addressed as *Tuan Haji*— *Tuan* being a minor honorific term used for Muslim dignitaries and government officials.

[3] *SSD*, 13 June 1886.

[4] *PCE*.

To sum up: the Sultan enjoyed a position of great dignity but not in most cases of great power. His dignity was related to his role as the apex of the political system of the State, as the symbol of its unity and the titular source of rank and authority for the chiefs among whom the real power was divided. The Sultan's dignity was buttressed by many attributes of sacredness and supernatural power. It was believed that he could influence the health and welfare of his subjects and the crops by which they lived. He exercised this influence by the passive fact of his existence and not by the performance of ritual. His dignity was given public recognition in the behaviour towards him of great chiefs in the political ceremonies in which the unity of the State was revalidated. Yet the chiefs lived in hostility with the Sultan and had little to do with him except in consultation and co-operation to preserve the State in its external relations, including its defence.

Apart from these national functions the Sultan was the chief of his own district. In his various functions he was assisted by a coterie of princes, chiefs and confidential advisers who were linked with him by personal ties and who were not representative of the general body of the chiefs. He had also a small number of writers and secretaries.

SUCCESSION TO THE SULTANATE

The royal office as the symbol of unity had to be above (i.e. out of the reach of) the major chiefs. On the other hand the Sultan would not be able to preserve unity unless he had some measure of acquiescence and loyalty from the chiefs or from most of them. The possibility of becoming Sultan was therefore confined to a single royal patrilineage distinct from the chiefly lineages. There was no automatic right of succession in favour of a son or younger brother of the late ruler. The choice of a successor from among the royal lineage rested with the chiefs. An aspirant to the throne had to court the support of the chiefs. A Sultan, at the start of his reign at least, had to be acceptable to the majority of the chiefs.

On the other hand a Sultan could usually advance the ablest of his sons to such prominence in his own lifetime that he would have a good chance of succeeding to the throne sooner or later. A Sultan was usually the son of a previous Sultan, but not necessarily of his immediate predecessor. This fact was reflected in the designation of sons, patrilineal grandsons and possibly nephews of any reigning or former Sultan as *waris negri* (heirs of the State). Effectively the choice of the chiefs was limited to the *waris negri*. Moreover, certain lesser royal offices were recognized as stepping stones to the Sultanate.

In these circumstances the personality of a candidate for the succession greatly affected his prospects. It was said of one Raja Yusuf who had several times been passed over by the chiefs of Perak that:

'He is stated to be obstinate, tyrannical and vindictive . . . the real objection
to him was that if they gave him power he would have had the will to wield it
and that they, therefore, preferred a weaker man. [1]

The fact that the system produced weak rulers was of course in keeping
with the distribution of power between Sultan and chiefs.

A second factor in the choice of a new Sultan was the status of his
mother. A man whose mother was of royal descent, especially if she was
the daughter of a Sultan, was preferred to a candidate who lacked this
advantage.[2] Sons who were royal by descent on both sides were known
as *anak gahara* or (in Perak) as *waris beneh dan tanah* (heirs by the seed
and the soil). It was usual for a Sultan to marry a woman of royal descent
as his first wife and royal consort (*Tunku Ampuan*). Sons, more especially
the eldest, of this union, had the best claim among the Sultan's children
to succeed. Sons by other wives were known as *anak gundek* (son of a
secondary wife). The basis of distinguishing a wife of inferior status
(*gundek*) was that either she was not royal or that she had not been married
with the ceremonies appropriate to a consort. There could not be more
than one royal consort.

The general principle underlying royal marriage alliances was the
tendency of office-holders to concentrate the succession among their own
descendants at the expense of collateral lines: e.g. an aspirant to the
throne, perhaps himself the son or close kinsman of a previous Sultan,
would marry the daughter of a reigning Sultan. He thus improved his
chances of succeeding to the throne since his father-in-law (though pre-
ferring his own sons) would support him against all other candidates. If
he did in fact become Sultan, his own sons would have a better chance
of succeeding in their turn because they were sons of a royal mother.
Through her the children would be related to another influential branch
of the royal dynasty since she might prove to be the sister and aunt as well
as the daughter of a Sultan.

The working of these tendencies is best illustrated by a review of the
actual succession to the Perak Sultanate in the nineteenth century. The
purpose of this review is to contrast the norm of what people said was
the rule for determining the succession with the actual practice, influenced by dominant personalities and by feud and intrigue in the ruling
class.

The Perak Sultans claimed patrilineal descent from a son of a Sultan
of Malacca who had come to Perak in the fifteenth century. During the
eighteenth century the pattern (which occurred twice in succession) was
that a Sultan was succeeded by each younger brother in turn. In the next
generation the sons of the last Sultan in the previous generation succeeded

---

[1] *SSD*, 19 August 1876.

[2] Winstedt (1947), p. 60: 'A Malay ruler's heir was . . . preferably the son of
a royal consort.'

in turn to the throne. The last of the second series was Sultan Ahmadin
who died in 1806. Thereafter the pattern changes[1]:

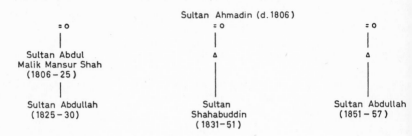

	Sultan Ahmadin (d. 1806)	
꞊ ○	꞊ ○	꞊ ○
Sultan Abdul	▵	▵
Malik Mansur Shah		
(1806–25)		
Sultan Abdullah	Sultan	Sultan Abdullah
(1825–30)	Shahabuddin	(1851–57)
	(1831–51)	

Only one of Sultan Ahmadin's three wives was royal by descent. But the
other two were daughters of chiefs and of high enough status to found
lines which shared in the succession. It thus became the recognized
norm[2] that the royal office should be held in turn by a member of the three
lines descended from Sultan Ahmadin and that the Sultan should be 'if
possible, the eldest legitimate son of a previous Sultan' of the branch
entitled on this occasion to fill the office. In practice there were numerous
irregularities:

(1) Raja Ahmad, a foreigner from Lingga (Rhio Archipelago), married
a daughter of Sultan Abdul Malik Mansur Shah (1806–25) and acquired
great influence. When it came round to the turn of this branch of the
royal lineage in 1857, a son of Raja Ahmad succeeded (as Sultan Ja'afar)
instead of a son of his brother-in-law Sultan Abdullah (1825–30). This
would appear to have been a breach of the rule of patrilineal descent.

(2) In the choice of successors to the Sultanate and other royal offices
in 1857, 1865, 1871 and 1874 the unpopular Raja Yusuf, son of Sultan
Abdullah (1851–7) was passed over.

(3) In 1871 the chiefs passed over the unpopular Raja Abdullah, son of
Sultan Ja'afar (1857–65), and elected as Sultan Raja Ismail who was
through his mother a great-great-grandson of an elder brother (and Sultan)
of Sultan Ahmadin. Again a breach of the patrilineal descent rule as also
of the rotation.

The fortunes of the three lines descended from Sultan Ahmadin can be
indicated as on page 57. The relationships mentioned are between the
individual and the previous Sultan of the same line.

It will be noted that Line 3 'missed its turn' twice in succession owing to
the unpopularity of Raja Yusuf. His ultimate accession was in fact due to
British support since, being ostracized from the ruling circle, he alone was
not implicated in the revolt known as the Perak War. Line 2 represented by

---

[1] Wilkinson and Winstedt (1934), p. 132.   [2] Swettenham (1948), p. 121.

Sultans of Perak 1825-1916

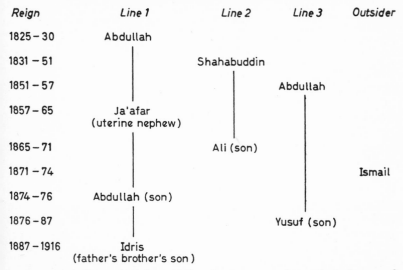

Reign	Line 1	Line 2	Line 3	Outsider
1825-30	Abdullah			
1831-51		Shahabuddin		
1851-57			Abdullah	
1857-65	Ja'afar (uterine nephew)			
1865-71		Ali (son)		
1871-74				Ismail
1874-76	Abdullah (son)			
1876-87			Yusuf (son)	
1887-1916	Idris (father's brother's son)			

an exceptionally weak Sultan (Ali), whose son was intermittently out of his mind, faded out completely. The tendency was always to divide the right to office so long as there was more than one strong line to contend for it and to eliminate the weaker lines in accordance with the balance of personalities of each generation.

The analysis on the previous three pages is confined to the inter-action of *descent*-lines and power politics. Affinal ties also played their part.[1] Sultan Abdullah, who became Raja Muda (Heir Apparent)[2] in 1865 was the son-in-law of Sultan Ali who acceded at that time. Idris who became Sultan in 1887 was the son-in-law of his predecessor, Sultan Yusuf. So much was the son-in-law of a Sultan equated with a son that leading authorities on Malay custom can say incidentally 'son of the reigning Sultan (a term often covering son-in-law)'.[3]

A more sustained example of the use of affinal ties to support claims to succeed to the Sultanate is provided by the Selangor situation (page 58): Abdul Samad, son of a younger son, married the daughter of his uncle, Sultan Mohamed, and displaced the Sultan's son, Mahmud, who was a minor, from the succession at Sultan Mohamed's death. Ten years later Abdul Samad, an easy-going man of sixty, decided to withdraw from public affairs and to delegate all his authority. In choosing a 'Viceroy' (Wakil Yam Tuan) he passed over his own sons and also the sons of his predecessor, Sultan Mohamed, and selected his son-in-law, Tunku Kudin, brother of the Sultan of the northern State of Kedah. He hoped that Kudin, a man of parts, would be acceptable as an impartial arbitrator

[1] See above, p. 55. [2] See below, p. 61. [3] Wilkinson and Winstedt (1934), p. 129.

E

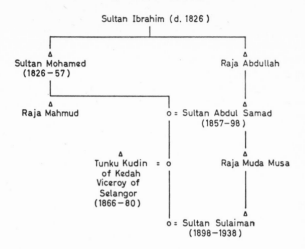

Sultan Ibrahim (d. 1826)

Sultan Mohamed (1826–57)

Raja Abdullah

Raja Mahmud

o = Sultan Abdul Samad (1857–98)

Tunku Kudin = o of Kedah Viceroy of Selangor (1866–80)

Raja Muda Musa

o = Sultan Sulaiman (1898–1938)

over the quarrels of the Selangor aristocrats (a hope which was disappointed). A generation later, in the calmer days of British rule, Sultan Abdul Samad's grandson and heir repeated the pattern by marrying a daughter of Tunku Kudin.

These episodes in dynastic history are an example of a more general problem which must arise in some form or another in any political system which enjoins the transmission of authority and high office according to rules based on kinship and descent. The significance of descent once admitted leads on to an elaboration of categories of nearer and remoter heirs, and in many cases to an absolute priority for some individual based on the accident of his birth. The odds are very much against the chosen heir being the most suitable candidate on personal grounds of his generation. The problem becomes acute when the system produces an heir who is entirely unsuitable. Malay history is not without examples of Sultans as despotic and insane as the Romans Caligula and Nero.[1] The system may nonetheless be rigid and admit of no solution except enforced abdication or assassination of a bad ruler. But many societies, including the Malay States, consciously imported a measure of flexibility to permit the exclusion of a bad candidate and even the choice of a good one (i.e. good from the point of view of the electors).

The principle of limiting the range of choice to a single descent group was not abandoned. There was some advantage in excluding the greater part of the ruling class from the possibility of succeeding to the throne.[2] Moreover, the tradition of Malay monarchy, upon which so much else of

[1] Wilkinson (1924), p. 45, describes Sultan Mahmud Shah II of Johore as 'having slain in the most fiendish manner those of his wives who had the misfortune to become pregnant'. He was murdered in 1699.

[2] See above, p. 54.

the values of the society depended, required that royalty, or at least the potentiality to become royal, should be based on descent. The conflicting principles of free choice of a suitable candidate and limitation to heirs born to their high estate were balanced in a rule that the heir must come from among members of the royal lineage.

The limited freedom of choice permitted by this rule (which is common enough in such situations) gave rise to its own problems. A lineage within which office is held branches out in each generation. Admittedly some branches become extinct in course of time. But in the absence of any strict rule such as primogeniture among male heirs there will always be more claimants to office than can ever hold it individually for life. This difficulty is relieved but not solved by instituting a system of rotation of office among branches of the lineage, such as developed in the Perak royal dynasty.[1] There is however, a contrary tendency at work. Members of the lineage who actually attain to office have a natural preference for transmitting their rights to their children in defiance of the principle of rotation[2]. It is usually beyond the ability of an individual office-holder, unless he is exceptionally powerful, to reserve the office to his descendants in exclusion of all other members of the lineage. But he and others who are closely associated with office-holding (as children of previous office-holders or as next in turn to hold office) tend to form an 'inner circle' which intermarries among itself and tries to exclude from office the newly developing collateral branches of each generation. In effect the rotation is confined within a small part of the lineage only.

In human society it is not sufficient to establish a monopoly of privilege. For the satisfaction of the privileged class and the discomfiture of rebels it is also necessary to justify the monopoly by arguments based on assumptions accepted by all. The 'inner circle' of the Malay royal lineage thus rationalized their claim by stressing the importance of near descent from an actual office-holder and of royal descent on both sides. The 'inner circle' intermarried. Granted that fact and the rationalization just stated, their practice of confining the Sultanate to their own children was above

[1] Rotation of office was much more widespread and elaborately organized in the Negri Sembilan clans (see above, p. 40). So far as the writer is aware rotation was quite unknown in the Malacca Sultanate and the Hindu kingdoms from which the Malay States inherited their tradition. As an hypothesis it may be supposed that rotation of office was a trait borrowed by the ruling class from the Menangkabau immigrants who became their subjects. Preoccupation with the number four in the organization of political groups was possibly another such borrowing.

[2] The desire to pass on one's rights and property to one's children would appear to be the result of conditioning to family life—even where physiological fatherhood is not known or admitted (Malinowski (1922), pp. 71–2). An aristocrat who acquires his status by descent has an additional reason for feeling that rights should be transmitted along descent lines.

criticism. None but their children had so many near ascendants who had held office. This was the qualification for office.[1]

Within the inner circle there was still need to build up one's own influence in superiority to others. Thus intermarriage was further used to cement the political alliances of the moment.

The existence and practices of the 'inner circle' were not often explicitly stated. But in Perak at least it was a group which was recognized by a special term (*waris negri*) for which there were known tests of membership and which carried the right to fill the lesser royal offices as well as the Sultanate. In 1882 under the British regime it was decided to pay allowances from public funds to the *waris negri* of Perak.[2] It was necessary to ask the State Council (the Sultan and the chiefs) to declare who were entitled to the allowances. The approved list included four sons, three daughters and seven sons' sons of previous Sultans and of the reigning Sultan. It also included Raja Idris, his three brothers and his four children as well as two other persons whose relationships cannot be determined. It is difficult to decide by what right Raja 'Dris and his kinsfolk were included. 'Dris was by descent a brother's son and a cousin of former Sultans and he was the son-in-law of the reigning Sultan by affinity. By way of achieved status he held the title of Raja Bendahara and, in the special circumstances of the time, was designated as the strongest candidate to succeed to the throne at the next vacancy. He did in fact become Sultan in 1887. The brothers of Raja 'Dris could not have been included merely as brothers of the Raja Bendahara. He and they must have ranked as *waris negri* because they were brother's sons of a former Sultan. Yet one finds no other brother's sons of Sultans included in the list and it is reasonable to suppose that such persons did exist. Secondly, it is notable that the children of Raja 'Dris were included but not the children of his brothers. It must be inferred that they were included as children of a Raja Bendahara and not as mere great-nephews and nieces of a former Sultan (a category which must have been numerous). In the ordinary way no one would attain to the office of Raja Bendahara unless, in contrast to Raja Idris, he was the son of a Sultan. It was an office indicating ultimate succession to the Sultanate too.[3] The children of a Raja Bendahara would ordinarily be grandchildren of a Sultan—and thus *waris negri* by reason of their grandfather. It must be concluded that *waris negri* was a term which, in keeping with the flexibility of the whole system, was variably interpreted. It was thus taken to include a son, a daughter, a son's son and a brother's son of any former Sultan and also the child of a Raja Muda or of a Raja Bendahara (in the rare cases where the males were not also grandsons of a former Sultan). Proximity to the throne in the male line was the crucial test.

[1] In Negri Sembilan the lustre of near descent on either side from the holder of a political office was expressed by the term *baka* and was explicitly recognized as a qualification for office.

[2] *P.S.C.*, 26 October, 1882.　　　　[3] See below, p. 62.

The close kinsmen of Sultans provided the holders of lesser royal offices. In many States the most important of these offices after the Sultanate itself was the office of Raja Muda. The title *Raja Muda* means either 'junior ruler' or 'future ruler',[1]—and both meanings were significant. With regard to the sense of 'future ruler' it must be stressed that there was no right of automatic succession to the Sultanate. The chiefs firmly resisted any attempt to settle irrevocably the choice of a successor before the death of the reigning Sultan. It was recognized however, that the Raja Muda had the right to be considered before any other candidate when the chiefs met in conclave to bury the late Sultan and to choose a new one. Nonetheless, a Raja Muda could be passed over.[2] In Perak and Selangor it rested with the chiefs to decide who should be advanced towards the Sultanate by becoming Raja Muda. In Perak, with its system of rotation of the Sultanate among three branches of the royal house, the Raja Muda was usually the son of a Sultan but not of the reigning Sultan. In Selangor he was the son of the reigning Sultan.

In Pahang the succession title was *Tengku Besar* (Chief Prince) instead of Raja Muda (this latter title, however, was used and was usually conferred on a younger brother of the reigning Sultan). In Negri Sembilan the royal office of Yam Tuan had been created by inviting over a Sumatran prince as ruler for life without any guarantee that the office would in due course descend to his heirs.[3] This tradition expressed the reluctance of the chiefs to submit to a royal ruler with any powers of internal administration. In conformity with this attitude the chiefs refused to recognize any office as conferring a claim to first consideration for the succession even though in the nineteenth century it was accepted that a successor would be chosen from the royal house of the late Yam Tuan. The Yam Tuan's son did indeed bear the title Tengku Besar but he could make no claim to the succession by virtue of that fact.

The second meaning of the title *Raja Muda* was 'junior ruler'. He was a deputy of the Sultan and he also acted as head of the members of the royal lineage as a group, thus standing between the Sultan and the royal house. The Raja Muda, like the Sultan, held a position of more dignity than power. For example, in Perak in the 1870's the chiefs denied the Raja Muda the right to collect certain customary revenues of his office in their districts.[4] A Raja Muda who tried to exert too much authority was likely to antagonize the chiefs and prejudice his chances of becoming Sultan later on. The chiefs did not favour the prospect of having a strong ruler.[5]

---

[1] Wilkinson (1932).

[2] It happened in Selangor in 1857, when the Raja Muda was a small boy, and in Perak in 1871 when the Raja Muda was absent from the royal funeral and unpopular with the electors, that another candidate was chosen as the new Sultan.

[3] See above, p. 16.   [4] See, e.g. Gullick (1953b), p. 26.

[5] See passage on Raja Yusuf of Perak quoted on p. 55 above. The chiefs for many years refused to elect Yusuf to any of the minor royal offices at all.

THE MINOR ROYAL OFFICES

In addition to the offices of Raja Muda or Tengku Besar, which stood next in dignity to the Sultanate, there were a number of minor offices held by members of the royal lineage who have close relatives of the Sultan. There was, for example, an office of *Tengku Panglima Besar* (royal commander-in-chief) in Selangor. In fact the Sultan had no army and the holder of the office was a confidant and executive assistant to the Sultan. In Negri Sembilan there was a corresponding office of *Tengku Panglima* with a corresponding lack of military functions. In Negri Sembilan there was also a *Tengku Laxamana* (royal admiral); in other States the Laxamana was usually a non-royal district chief.

The most important of all these lesser offices was the Raja Bendahara of Perak. In the Malacca Sultanate the Bendahara was the greatest of the Sultan's ministers; not himself of royal descent but often the father-in-law or brother-in-law of the Sultan. In nineteenth-century Perak, however, the office of Bendahara had been appropriated by the royal lineage and bore the prefix *Raja Bendahara*. It had ceased to have any ministerial functions and had become a royal office of dignity second only to the Sultan and the Raja Muda. This situation reflected the arrangement[1] that the Sultan of Perak should be drawn in turn from each of three branches of the royal house. The reigning sultan came from branch 'A'; his half-designated successor, the Raja Muda, came from branch 'B' which stood next in turn to provide a Sultan; branch 'C' provided the Raja Bendahara. In theory on the death of the Sultan the Raja Muda became Sultan and branch 'B' thus had its turn in the rotation of the Sultanate. The Raja Bendahara of the previous reign moved up to become Raja Muda; branch 'C' of the royal house thus had its turn in providing a Raja Muda and moved on towards providing the Sultan of the next reign. The office of Raja Bendahara, thus vacated, was filled by a member of branch 'A' of the royal house, usually a son of the late Sultan; branch 'A' thus re-entered the cycle at the bottom end. These appointments rested with the chiefs and, as has been explained, the practice did not always conform strictly to the norm, which was itself no more than two generations old. The actual sequence in Perak was as follows:

Period	Sultan	Raja Muda	Raja Bendahara
1857–65	Ja'afar (A)	Ali (B)	Ismail (outsider)
1865–71	Ali (B)	Abdullah (A)	Ismail (outsider)
1871–74	Ismail (outsider)	Abdullah (A)	Osman (B)
1874–76	Abdullah (A)	Yusuf (C)	Osman (B)
1876–87	—	Yusuf (C)	Idris (A)

[1] See above, p. 56.

The noticeable irregularities of actual practice did not extinguish the memory of what the true norm was. On the other hand no one (except disappointed candidates) asserted that any of the irregular appointments were invalid because they were irregular. It was recognized that the chiefs had discretion in their choice.[1]

Relations between the Sultan and his close kinsmen were not usually cordial. There was a great deal of jealousy and recrimination about the right to fill royal offices (and thus enter the succession sequence to the Sultanate) and about the sharing of royal revenues.

The royal consort and lesser wives of the Sultan played no part in the government and had no political influence except in those cases where a woman of strong character or influential connexions intrigued to advance the interests of her sons. The royal wives did not take any great part in the ceremonial and ritual of the royal house. The royal consort was usually herself of royal descent. The lesser wives were not royal but were related to men of position, e.g. Sultan Abdullah of Perak had married the daughter of a previous Sultan as his consort. One of his secondary wives was the sister of the two leading Bugis adventurers and business men of quasi-aristocratic status in Perak at that time.

THE ROYAL HOUSEHOLD

It was the Malay custom to provide each wife with her own house. Sultans also had, or were supposed to have, a principal residence or palace (*Astana*). A new *Astana* was to be built for each Sultan. In practice some nineteenth-century Sultans could not command the resources needed to construct a palace of suitable size. Sultan Ali of Perak (1865–71) lodged with a district chief during the whole of his reign.[2] Sultan Abdullah of Perak (1874–6) on his accession lived for a time in the house of Haji Musa, a wealthy headman of the village of Batak Rabit. A visitor noted that:

'The Sultan's place is hardly worthy of his high rank, in fact his house is set upon the weed and a more vile, slippery place I never saw.'[3]

Later on in his short reign fear of an epidemic caused him to move and he seems to have lived in a boat for quite long periods. When a Sultan died his successor had to find some other abode. The late Sultan's palace could be used for the accommodation of visitors but not as a permanent dwelling place.[4] On the layout of royal and other aristocratic dwellings something is said in a later section.[5]

[1] The irregularity began with the passing over of Raja Yusuf in 1857. As son of the late Sultan he should have been appointed Bendahara. Owing to his unpopularity the chiefs appointed Ismail, a member of the royal house only on his mother's side, in his place. Ismail, owing to his doubtful status, remained as Bendahara in 1865 and Abdullah, son of the late Sultan Ja'afar, became Raja Muda direct. Subsequent events were pure power politics.

[2] Swettenham (1951), p. 49.   [3] *ibid.*, p. 42.

[4] *SSD*, 20 August 1887.   [5] See below, pp. 109–12.

The chiefs and royal kinsmen who were in attendance on the Sultan for short or long periods found their own accommodation. If they had arrived by boat for a short visit it was quite common for them to live in their boats during their stay. The Sultan's household consisted of secretaries, armed retainers, domestic servants, boatmen, watchmen and concubines. A Sultan's harem could be relatively large. Sultan Abdullah of Perak once took eleven concubines in his suite on a journey. The Sultan of Pahang was reputed to have a harem of 300–400 women.[1] The size of the royal household was swelled by a number of the destitute and of fugitives from the justice of chiefs seeking sustenance and asylum under the Sultan's protection. The maintenance of these refugees was a heavy burden.[2] It was also a source of prestige and a subject of proverbial wisdom.[3]

As examples of the size of a Sultan's household, there is the case of Sultan Abdullah travelling in four boats—one for himself, one for his wife, one for his concubines and one for his cooks and domestics. On another occasion, as a demonstration of force he travelled with fifty boats and 500 men. At one of his entertainments the number of domestics was apparently insufficient for handing round the food and his secretaries were pressed into service. It is probable that except on warlike occasions a Sultan probably had a residential household of no more than fifty persons. The number of his dependants who 'lived out' was a considerable addition.

Members of the Sultan's household enjoyed prestige by their association with their master. Musicians of the royal band, elephant mahouts, magicians, etc. of the royal household in Kedah were exempt from the general obligation to do manual labour (*kerah*) when required.[4] To assault a slave of the royal household in Pahang was an offence punishable with death. Seduction of a concubine of the Sultan's harem entailed torture and death for both parties. The special position of menial members of the royal household was correlated with the dignity and sacredness of the ruler.

[1] *AR Phg*, 1889.   [2] See below, p. 128.

[3] e.g. 'The larger the cooking pot, the more the rice which sticks to the inside of it' (*Besar periok, besar kerak-nya*), Brown (1951), p. 29.

[4] *AR Kedah*, 1909.

4

The Ruling Class

THE CLASS SYSTEM

The division of the community into two classes—a ruling class and a subject class—was one of the basic elements of Malay political and social structure. 'The people had no initiative whatever', said Swettenham.[1] A man of common birth expressed his relations with his chief as follows:

'I was one of the Maharaja Lela's followers. I must do what he bids me. I am his *ra'ayat* (subject). I would not dare to resist him.'[2]

There were no doubt exceptions to a greater or less extent (the most important being the situation in Negri Sembilan[3]) but the known facts bear out the general accuracy of the proposition that leadership and control in all aspects of Malay life—political, legal, military and (to a lesser extent) economic and ritual—tended to be concentrated in the ruling class.

The distinction between the two classes was strictly marked. Intermarriage was disapproved—in the upper class. It was almost impossible for a commoner to rise into the ruling class of the State in which he had been born and where his antecedents were known. Collections of Malay proverbs teem with disapprobation of the attempted upstart, the bean who forgets the pod (of his origin).[4] The approved conduct is to consort and intermarry with one's equal—hornbill with hornbill and sparrow with sparrow.[5] It is folly for a commoner to stand up against his betters like a soft cucumber fighting a prickly durian.[6] The wise man bows to authority—'whoever may be king, I'll knuckle my forehead to him'.[7]

THE RULING CLASS

The ruling class was an institution closely related to the Sultanate. It included many persons of royal descent who were too remotely related

[1] Swettenham (1948), p. 141.

[2] *SSD*, 10 January 1877. The Maharaja Lela was on trial for murder and it was perhaps natural that his subjects should stress his responsibility for the act in which they were all implicated.

[3] See above, pp. 39–41, especially p. 41. Also see below, pp. 74–9.

[4] *Kachang lupakan kulit.* Winstedt (1950), p. 36, where six other proverbs to the same effect are quoted.

[5] *Enggang sama enggang, pipit sama pipit.* Brown (1951), p. 34.

[6] *Bagai mentimun dengan durian.* Brown, op. cit. p. 95.

[7] *Siapa jadi raja, tahan aku ka-dahi juga.* Brown, op. cit., p. 94.

to any Sultan to be able to aspire to the throne or the lesser royal offices. The non-royal members of the ruling class derived their status indirectly from the Sultanate. These men could not aspire to the throne or claim royal descent. But they were aristocrats by virtue of membership of lineages whose claim to high status depended on their right to fill various chieftainships. The chiefs were appointed by the Sultan and their offices were graded in classes of descending order of seniority based on the origin of the titles in the time of the Malacca Sultans when they were held not by chiefs but by royal ministers. Negri Sembilan however was something of an exceptional case.

The ruling class of each state was a separate group from the corresponding class of any other State. They recognized each other's status as equal to their own but intermarriage across State frontiers was almost unknown.

The Sultan of the State was thus the apex of the ruling class, the symbol of the unity of the group and the point of reference by which, directly or indirectly through chieftainships, the members of the ruling class determined their relative status. The concept of differential status was one of the main interests and values of the ruling class.

Two main elements in the ruling class—junior branches of the royal lineage and the lineages of chiefs—have already been mentioned incidentally. The third, and less important, element comprised persons absorbed into the ruling class and not born into it. A description is now given of each element.

THE OUTER FRINGE OF THE ROYAL LINEAGE

Everyone of either sex descended in the male line from a Sultan bore a title of royal status as a personal prefix to his or her name. In Perak and Selangor this title was Raja; e.g. Raja Mohamed, Raja Khatijah. In Negri Sembilan the title was *Tunku*.[1] So long as there was unbroken descent in the male line all children bore the appropriate title as a birthright. Moreover the son of a Sultan, unless some special royal title had been conferred on him as an office (e.g. Raja Bendahara), was entitled to no other prefix to his name (than 'Raja') which would distinguish him from the great-grandson of some former Sultan.

If a woman of royal descent married a man of non-royal descent, her children did not inherit the title of royal status.[2] Such a marriage was considered a 'social degradation' to the woman.[3] A male member of the royal lineage however could transmit royal descent status to his children

---

[1] More correctly but less often spelt *Tengku*.

[2] There was a title *Megat* to indicate royal descent through the mother but it was only rarely and irregularly used. See Wilkinson (1932) and Winstedt (1947b), p. 42.

[3] Winstedt (1947b), p. 41.

by a non-royal wife. Nonetheless it was usual for a male 'Raja' to take a woman of his own descent status as his first or principal wife. If he took a second wife of non-royal status, the wedding ceremony was of the type which indicated a secondary union. In these circumstances marriages between male Rajas and daughters of non-royal chiefs were not common. A woman of distinguished but non-royal descent could do better for herself by becoming the principal wife of a chief who might well have greater wealth and influence than many a Raja.

The preference of minor members of the royal lineage for marrying a principal wife of their own descent status is easily explained. A 'Raja' on the outer fringe of the royal dynasty might have little hope of holding the Sultanate or any of the offices around the throne. But he still looked to the Sultanate as the origin of his own exalted status and to the circle around the throne as the model of his conduct. Accordingly he sought, as they did, to beget children of the highest possible royal status and accepted their standard, viz. that royal descent on the maternal as well as the paternal side conferred higher status than patrilineal royal descent alone. In his case the choice of a wife of royal descent as the mother of his children served no useful purpose (as it did for the 'inner circle'[1]) except perhaps to produce the esteem which always results from strict conformity with the code of the group to which one belongs. It is an interesting example of how a value developed as a justification for a particular set of circumstances can be adopted by people to whom the circumstances do not apply but who would like to identify themselves with those persons to whom the circumstances do apply. In more direct terms 'aping one's betters' is its own reward.

The royal lineage accepted one group of outsiders as equal in status to themselves. These were the descendants of the Prophet Mohamed who bore the personal prefix before their names of 'Syed' (if male) and 'Sharifa' (if female). There was no stigma of disapproval or loss of status attached to a marriage between a female 'Raja' and a 'Syed' (nor between a 'Sharifa' and a male 'Raja' though this seems to have been less common). Many of the Syeds were Indonesian immigrants, especially from Acheh in north Sumatra, who came to the Malay States and married into the ruling class. British administrators later on blamed the 'Arab half-breed element' for the disturbances of the period before the Malay States came under British protection.[2] It is certain at least that Syeds played a considerable part in the war and intrigue of the early 1870's in Selangor and Negri Sembilan. Many of them, although accepted as royal, were rather needy adventurers who lived by their wits.

[1] See above, pp. 55 and 57–60.

[2] *AR NS*, 1892. Lister was probably referring to the Syeds who became district chiefs of Tampin and of Sungei Ujong. In Selangor (in which Lister had served) Syed Mashhor, son of an Arab and a Malay woman of Pontianak (Borneo) was a noted war-leader.

The Raja element in the ruling class held itself aloof in the matter of intermarriage and reckoned itself a cut above the non-royal aristocrats. But in fact they were assimilated in status to those aristocrats. In Selangor the situation took an extreme form—the royal lineage took over all the district chieftainships and ousted the non-royal lineages completely. The same tendency appeared in Negri Sembilan where branches of the royal family became established (not without fighting) in Tampin and in Jelebu. Even in Perak certain members of the royal house had carved out districts for themselves. The unpopular Raja Yusuf[1] controlled the district of Senggang on the Perak River and Raja Idris was chief of Kampar (a side valley). The two groups, royal and non-royal, at no time formed themselves into compact and hostile opponents, but there was always an element of individual competition in the sense that they were all competing for a limited number of opportunities to rule districts.

THE NON-ROYAL LINEAGES

In a note at the end of this chapter is a review of the district chieftainships of Perak, Selangor and Negri Sembilan. These chieftainships were the offices of authority around which the ruling class was organized into lineages.

Before describing the lineages which formed the bulk of the Malay ruling class it seems necessary to discuss the nature of lineages. Much of what follows is generally true of the royal lineage of each State as well as of the non-royal lineages. Negri Sembilan is, as always, a rather exceptional situation; there the non-royal lineages were based on matrilineal descent and the gap between ruling class and subject class was less clear-cut.

The aggregation of groups (on a larger scale than the family) on the basis of unilineal descent can serve different purposes. Lineage structure varies with function. For the purpose of making certain distinctions in the structure of Malay aristocratic lineages it suffices to contrast them with a different type of lineage of which much has been written. This contrasted type of lineage is exemplified in the Nuer and in the Tallensi societies. In these cases the lineages, or the genealogical trees which express the pattern of the lineages, serve as a framework by which small groups are set in a permanent relationship of balanced opposition within a larger group to which the smaller groups acknowledge that they belong (in contrast to members of other larger groups to which their own larger group is opposed). There is thus a social tension and a set form by which the whole community is held together. The actual genealogies of real descent are reformulated and foreshortened so as to provide a pattern of putative descent to correspond with the existing hierarchy from minimal up to maximal lineages. Such a system is usually associated with an

[1] See above, pp. 55 and 56.

absence of organs of purely political authority. It exists to provide a charter for the balanced opposition of groups by which order is maintained.

By contrast lineages can serve the needs of a political system of a very different kind in which there are offices of authority, and status is dependent on lineal connexion with the holders of such offices. In such cases lines of descent are used to set everyone in his appointed place and to define provisionally or finally what is his entitlement to political authority. It is suggested that the Malay aristocratic lineage was an example of this type of lineage, which is also to be found in Polynesia, Indonesia and in some tribes of Africa.

In this type of lineage (hereafter referred to as the 'status lineage' in contrast to the other type of 'segmentary lineage') there are offices of political authority which can generally be styled chieftainships. Initiative and authority of various kinds is exercised by chiefs in co-operation with a considerable number of lesser leaders and organizers. The lineage system is made the charter of status for members of the directing group of the society. A chieftainship, and possibly some lesser and ancillary offices, are made the hereditary perquisite of a group of kinsmen related by common unilineal descent. Only one member at a time of each lineage can hold the chieftainship. A few of the other members hold minor offices. The majority merely claim (and exercise the prerogatives of) status as members of the lineage. The claim can be broken down into two elements. First, there is a claim to group status as a member of a corporation which has a collective right to provide the holder of a particular office or group of offices of dignity and authority. Secondly, there is a claim to personal status by descent, close or remote, from an actual holder of the office of authority.

The emphasis and social interest of the status lineage does not lie in segmentation into small opposed groups. The significant factor is proximity to or remoteness from the present holder of the office or one of his predecessors. The 'inner circle'[1] of the Malay royal lineage provides an example. The outer fringe of the royal lineage remained royal but less so.

A more elaborate example is provided by the title system of Javanese royalty. In this case the son of a Sultan bears the title 'Pangeran'. Patrilineal descendants down to great-grandsons (unless promoted as individuals) bear the title 'Raden Mas'. Remoter patrilineal descendants are styled 'Raden' only.

It is convenient to contrast the different functions of a 'status lineage' and a 'segmentary lineage', each being treated as an abstraction of a particular tendency. But it would be wrong to treat the distinction as absolute and to classify any particular lineage system as wholly and only of one type or the other. It is rather a question of classifying a particular case as predominantly of one type or the other but containing traces at least of the opposite type.

[1] See above, p. 59.

Thus there are distinct indications of the segmentary or opposed group pattern in the Malay lineage system. The choice of a new chief to fill the lineage office when it fell vacant gave rise to opposed trends of group unity and fission. The first phase was the determination of the question whether the vacant office would be filled again by a member of the same lineage as the previous holders. A non-royal lineage in Perak considered itself entitled to provide a successor whenever an office held by one of its members fell vacant. But the power to appoint a chief rested with the Sultan and the expectation of the lineage was not automatically fulfilled. Each chieftainship was in practice associated with the right to administer a district. The district chief's lineage was established as the leading family of the district. If however the lineage had lost influence in its district or if the district had waned in importance, the Sultan might appoint a new chief from a different lineage or leave the office vacant and allow the chief of a neighbouring district to absorb the vacant fief in his own.[1] During this phase the lineage was united.

The second phase or situation (not necessarily subsequent in time to the first) tended to divide the lineage internally into opposing factions. Supposing it was not in doubt that the vacant office was to be filled by a member of the same lineage as before, the question remained—which individual among several in the lineage? There was no rule of automatic succession. The son (by the principal wife) of the late chief or his younger brother had a better claim to succeed than anyone else but might be passed over in favour of a remoter kinsman.

Some lineages developed a system of rotation of the chieftainship among branches of the lineage on lines similar to the rotation of the Perak Sultanate.[2] Apart from the necessity of sharing privilege among two or more branches because no one branch could dominate the rest, rotation of office must tend to develop in a situation where, as in the Malay States, a younger brother is almost as strong a claimant as a son. In such circumstances it must sometimes happen that the younger brother does succeed and the son is passed over. When the younger brother dies the succession is likely to be disputed between the son of the elder brother who was chief first and the son of the younger brother who has just died. (See diagram top of page 71.)

This situation occurred in the Negri Sembilan royal family in 1869 and the succession was in dispute for six years afterwards. The son of the younger brother (D) may give way to the son of the older brother (C)

[1] In 1862 the office of *Mentri* of Perak was taken away from a lineage in decline which had held it for a century and given to the upstart chief of Larut. In 1871 the Dato' Panglima Bukit Gantang, in whose district Larut had been included until it was made a separate district, died. The office was left vacant thereafter because the all-powerful Mentri of Larut then overshadowed all that part of Perak. The rise of the chiefs of Larut at the expense of their neighbours was remarkable but not unique.

[2] See above, p. 56.

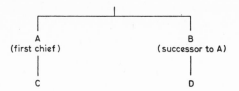

on condition that he (D) is to succeed (C) in due course. The course of the succession of the office of Dato' Panglima Kinta (of Perak) is an example:[1]

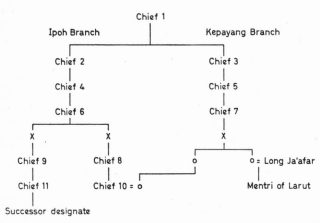

The eventual exclusion of the Kepayang branch was no doubt due to loss of influence. Thereupon a new rotation (more strictly 'alternation' in this case) developed inside the Ipoh branch itself, indicating the essentially structural nature of the arrangement. Affinal ties are shown only for recent times. It will be noted that the Kepayang branch, although excluded from the chieftainship married back into the line of chiefs and also made an alliance with the rising family of the chiefs of Larut.[2]

In Selangor the situation was different in that the royal lineage held all the district chieftainships. But the same tendency to fission appeared whenever the question of appointing a new district chief arose. There was a conflict between the inclination of the Sultan (or his more powerful backers) to concentrate power and office in the hands of his close kinsmen and the contrary tendency of collateral branches of the royal lineage to appropriate a district chieftainship, once obtained, as a hereditary fief to be held by the same line for ever. Selangor consisted of five districts, each a separate valley running down to the sea. The two outlying districts

---

[1] *PSC*, 1880–2, Appendix. Chief 11 was in office in 1909.

[2] The significance of intermarriage between chiefly families is considered later. See below, pp. 83 ff.

at the extreme north and south had become the hereditary fiefs of two collateral branches of the royal lineage. In the three central districts (Selangor, Klang and Langat) the situation was more fluid and gave rise to a celebrated quarrel in the 1860's. In the reign of Sultan Mohamed the Klang district had been assigned to his son, Raja Sulaiman. At the death of Raja Sulaiman his son, Raja Mahdi, claimed to succeed to his father's district. The real power rested with a wealthy chief, Raja Juma'at, who persuaded the Sultan to give the Klang district to one Raja Abdullah, a brother of Raja Juma'at. Although Raja Mahdi was the old Sultan's grandson, he represented an offshoot from the circle around the Sultan headed by the all-powerful, Raja Juma'at. It was a conflict between the tendency to concentrate power in one line and the tendency to divide it between several lines:

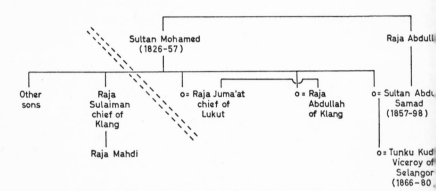

The double broken line indicates the opposition between 'haves' to the right and 'have nots' to the left. The 'haves' were a coalition of outsiders associated only by affinal ties. Raja Abdullah and Raja Juma'at were sons of a member of the Rhio branch of the royal lineage and were regarded as outsiders by the local-born faction. Tunku Kudin was a brother of the Sultan of Kedah. In the civil war of 1866–73 one faction was led by Tunku Kudin and included the sons of Raja Abdullah of Klang; the other was led by Raja Mahdi and included to a greater or less extent all the sons of Sultan Mohamed and of Sultan Abdul Samad. Irregular as the situation is, it shows the tendency of a group around the throne to exclude the wider group of members of the lineage from the fruits of power and office.

It would be an exaggeration to apply the term 'medial lineage' to these factions in the Perak and Selangor lineages. They were irregular in structure and they had no formal or enduring composition. The groups competing for office in each generation formed around the strong candidates of the time. But it must be taken into account that a member of a lineage who had no hope of obtaining office himself usually lent his support to his *closest* kinsman who was 'in the running'. The apparently ephemeral coalitions were to some extent based on ties of common descent in the same line of lineage. To that extent it was an opposition between segments. But much depended on the character, wealth, influence and other personal characteristics of the candidates.

At this point it is convenient to discuss relations between office-holders (i.e. chiefs) and the 'rank and file' of the lineages from which they came. It happened only once in a period of years that the lineage was united and divided by the sequence of events which occurred in choosing a new chief. In the intervals when there was a chief in office reciprocal ties of self-interest held the lineage together around the chief. A chief needed the help of his kinsmen in the administration of his district and also for its defence. He could in theory have obtained such help from outsiders. But it is indicative of the importance of kinship ties in the political system that the chief did in fact recruit his helpers from among his lineage. On their side the members of the lineage needed a patron who would protect them if they fell foul of another chief and who would afford them the opportunity of making a living. Thus it usually happened that a chief had in his retinue a number of kinsmen who managed his property, acted as confidential adviser (and sometimes as secretary), assisted in the work of government, commanded the chief's bodyguard and collected his taxes. In return these helpers were given their keep and were either granted an allowance from the chief's resources or were tacitly allowed to make what they could from the opportunities of their position. In many cases the kinsman expected and received no more than the right to trade, to mine for tin or to set up a local toll-station somewhere in the district.

It seems frequently to happen that the relationship between two roles in a situation contains elements which conflict. In this case it was not a simple situation of reciprocal interest between chief and kinsman. There was also a conflict of interest. The chief naturally sought to advance his sons in the work of government at the expense of his collateral relatives. The succession to office after his death was thus more likely to go to his son.[1] Collateral kinsmen were helpers for the moment but potential rivals to the chief's sons.

Secondly there was some conflict over the sharing of the revenues which the chief could collect in the district under his control. He wanted to keep as much as possible for himself. His kinsmen if dissatisfied had a recognized right to bring pressure to bear by pillaging and causing disturbance among the peasantry of the district, e.g.

'A petty chief and his adherents being in disgrace with the Sultan thus avenge

---

[1] As an example of the importance of building up influence and a connexion there is the episode related by Swettenham (1951), pp. 50 and 77, of the choice of a new Sri Adika Raja of Upper Perak. One candidate was a son of the late chief. But the Sultan preferred a collateral kinsman who had more local support in the Upper Perak District.

F

themselves on their weaker brethren but should they again be taken into favour they become exemplary members of society.'[1]

As an example of such pressure on a district chief there is the case of two cousins of the Mentri of Larut (in Perak) who, being denied their previous allowance of $200 p.m. from the Mentri, set up in opposition to levy taxes for themselves at Kurau far away to the north of the Larut district.[2] The expression *mengamok* was used of forays of this kind.[3]

NEGRI SEMBILAN IN CONTRAST TO PERAK AND SELANGOR

The Negri Sembilan lineages were of a mixed type between the status lineage and the segmentary lineage. There were chieftainships as the basis of lineage status. The lineages were formally and permanently divided into segments. It was not a clear-cut contrast with Perak and Selangor but rather a change of emphasis. The lineages of Perak and Selangor were status lineages with tendencies towards irregular and temporary segmentation over such questions as succession to the chieftainships. In Negri Sembilan the same tendencies existed for the same reasons; partly for historical reasons[4] they had become a formally recognized and structural feature of the lineage system.

The Negri Sembilan political system has already been described.[5] The royal lineage was weaker than in the other States and it was in sharper opposition to the non-royal ruling class. By contrast with the other States there was also a lack of unity in the ruling class. For in Perak and Selangor, although there was opposition between the chiefs and the lineages which they represented, there was also intermarriage between lineages and a general recognition by the ruling class of its own existence as a single if loosely co-ordinated group. In Negri Sembilan the centrifugal forces were stronger. Each district was a separate political unit in which hostility to neighbouring districts was the normal state of affairs. Intermarriage between districts was not common.

The most obvious contrast between the Negri Sembilan ruling class (other than the royal lineage) and the corresponding class in other States

---

[1] *SSD*, 6 April 1875.   [2] *SSD*, 10 July 1873.

[3] *Mengamok* is familiar in English as 'running amuck'. It is usually taken to refer to the case of a Malay peasant whose release from intolerable oppression was to murder everyone he met until hunted down to death like an animal. But *amok* also means to attack recklessly. It was thus used of an aristocratic marauder preying on a society which denied him a legitimate income. The essential ideas are (1) an intense sense of grievance and (2) indiscriminate and murderous violence against society—not necessarily against the individuals responsible for the grievance.

[4] See pp. 37–42. The lineages were made up by aggregation rather than broken down by division. The segment had always had recognition as a structural unit.

[5] See pp. 16 and 38–40.

was the fact that the Negri Sembilan lineages were matrilineal descent groups. A second major point of contrast was the absence in Negri Sembilan of a clear-cut and formally recognized dividing line between the ruling class. and their subjects. This was however a difference of degree rather than an absolute contrast. In Negri Sembilan eligibility for political office and intermarriage with the families of office-holders was confined within a minority group. The unprivileged majority, although organized as client lineages around the nucleus of the ruling group, was of lower status. The position of the ruling group was defined by such expressions as *berpesaka* (entitled to office) and *waris menyandang* (heirs to office). But it was not a topic of major social interest—in contrast to the *Raja/Ra'ayat* situation of the other States. One of the most significant means of differentiating status in Negri Sembilan was the test of the amount of the marriage payment (*mas kahwin*). For example in Sungei Ujong the payment was $48 when the bride was a woman of the clan of the district chief, $24 if she was a member of one of the other privileged lineages and $12 in other cases. The hangings, pillows, awnings, etc. used as decorations at weddings, funerals and other major occasions were also limited by a graded scale according to the status of the family.

The exclusion of the later immigrant groups from participation in the chieftainships and clan headships was correlated with an indifference on their part to the succession disputes of the ruling group. A British officer reporting on the election of the Dato' Klana (district chief) of Sungei Ujong in 1880 wrote:

> 'Outside the circle of the Waris and the electory Dato's there appeared to me an utter indifference as to who might become Klana.'[1]

In this respect there is an interesting contrast between Negri Sembilan and Perak and Selangor. In all three States there were two contrasted principles of alignment. There was a 'horizontal' cleavage into rulers and subjects; there was also a 'vertical' division into districts in which the interests of the subject population were to some extent identified with those of their local aristocrats. In Perak and Selangor the 'horizontal' division was the dominant one; in Negri Sembilan the 'vertical' division into districts was more marked and (in the eyes of the people themselves) more significant. It is rather surprising that in States where the horizontal distinction was more important the bond of local loyalty (a loyalty defined by the vertical division) of subject class to their district chief was stronger. The peasants of Perak and Selangor seem to have had much more of an emotional attachment to their chiefs than was the case in the more egalitarian situation of Negri Sembilan.

THE NEGRI SEMBILAN LINEAGES

Within the ruling class of each district there was an elaborate lineage structure based on the balanced opposition of groups. The details varied

[1] *SSD*, 3 March 1880.

a great deal between one district and another but certain general features can be distinguished.

In most cases the major line of division[1] was between (1) the clan (known as the *Waris*) from which the district chief (*Undang*) and some lesser officers (*orang besar*) were drawn and (2) the clans of Sumatran immigrants (*suku*) from whose privileged lineages the clan headmen (*lembaga*) were drawn. This contrast reflected a real clash of authority. The clan headmen as a group held the district chief in check and insisted, so far as they were able, that he must consult them and deal with their clansmen through them and not directly. This opposition was expressed in proverbs; e.g. the district chief has authority over all his district, the clan headman only over the members of his clan.[2]

In these clashes the district chief relied on the backing of his own *Waris* clan against the headmen of the immigrant *Suku*. The two opposed groups were, in form, of different status (the *Waris* being the higher) and origin. In its working however the system developed into a balance of like groups expressed through dissimilar offices. This view of the matter is reinforced by the situation in Sungei Ujong where, a unique case in Negri Sembilan, the major line of cleavage was not between *Waris* and *Suku* but between two sections of the *Waris* itself. In Sungei Ujong (less subject to Menangkabau influence than other parts of Negri Sembilan) the *Waris* clan was so much in control that an internal split developed within the *Waris* clan itself. There was in fact a division of the office of district chief between two chiefs who held it in commission.[3] Each chief was drawn from and supported by his own segment of the *Waris*. The two segments were the '*Waris* by land' (*Waris di-Darat*) and the '*Waris* by water' (*Waris di-Ayer*). These terms meant no more than a division by locality, i.e. *Waris di-Darat* lived further up the Linggi River than *Waris di-Ayer* who were nearer the sea. The two chiefs each ruled their own people and were too often at loggerheads to sustain even a fiction of joint incumbency of a single office. It is interesting therefore that the adages of the Sungei Ujong constitution continued to assert that:

'Like a single egg supported on the palms of two hands, a single office is nourished between two.'[4]

It may be inferred that despite the division into two opposed groups there was felt to be an essential unity. The district was complete only by comprising both halves:

'When di-Darat is lost, di-Ayer must search;
When di-Ayer is lost, di-Darat must search.'[5]

[1] See diagram on p. 42 and the explanation leading up to it.

[2] A free translation of *Undang berkelantasan, lembaga bersekat*.

[3] The anomalous position in Sungei Ujong is discussed in Gullick (1949), at pp. 30–7.

[4] *Telor sa-biji sama di-tatang, satu pesaka sama di-bela.*

[5] *Hilang di-Darat, di-Ayer mencharikan, hilang di-Ayer, di-Darat mencharikan.* Quoted with reference to the election of a new chief when either office is vacant.

Elsewhere in Negri Sembilan where the main division was between *Waris* and *Suku* there was the same sentiment that both elements were necessary complements to each other in making up the social unit of the district (known in Negri Sembilan as *Luak*).

Below the level of major division, of whatever kind, there was a system of internal segmentation within each clan. In discussing the situation in Perak and Selangor it has been argued that a lineage associated with the filling of an office must tend to split internally over the choice of a candidate to fill the office (whenever the succession question arises and often in anticipation of such occasions). In Negri Sembilan this tendency to fission had found expression in structural (as distinct from occasional and irregular) sub-division of clans. Thus the *Waris* clan which provided the district chief of its district was divided into a number of segments each of which usually traced its descent from a child of the first legendary district chief. There were three such segments in Jelebu. In Rembau there were no less than eight segments (organized into two opposed coalitions of four each—a less developed manifestation of the situation already described in Sungei Ujong). In theory the right to provide a district chief passed by rotation round the circle of segments.[1] Thus in the Rembau system just mentioned the Undang was supposed to be taken in turn from each of the two major groupings and within each grouping there was a rule that the four segments should also share office in turn:

GROUP X		GROUP Y	
Segment A	1st turn	Segment E	2nd turn
,, B	3rd ,,	,, F	4th ,,
,, C	5th ,,	,, G	6th ,,
,, D	7th ,,	,, H	8th ,,

But the strict order of rotation was not observed even when there was no dispute (as there often was) as to the correct order itself.

The immigrant clans (*Suku*), like the *Waris*, were divided into segments which shared by rotation in the clan headship.

In all cases a vacant office was filled by election. The electors were the heads of the groups below the office to be filled. The electors were confined (in theory at least) to choosing a candidate from the segment eligible to fill the office on this occasion. In fact there was a wrangle in two stages. There was first a dispute as to which segment was next in turn to fill the office. This question settled, there was much intrigue by individuals in the eligible group to canvass the support of the electors. In theory the choice had to be by unanimous choice of the electors. In practice a disagreement was resolved either by fighting or by the grudging acquiescence of the weaker faction.

Apart from intrigue and pure power politics there were other ways of circumventing the rules of rotation among segments. A district chief or

[1] For this rule there was inevitably an adage: *pesaka bergilir*—office inherited by descent rotates.

clan head could usually marry a woman of the segment from which his own successor must come and thus beget a son eligible to succeed when he himself died. Alternatively he might marry the daughter or sister of one of the electors and hope that a son born of this union would succeed owing to the influence of his maternal grandfather or uncle despite any rules of rotation to the contrary. The tendency of chiefs and clan headmen to confine the succession to their own descendants found expression in a rule that a candidate's proximity in *either* line of descent to a former office-holder (not necessarily a holder of the same office) gave him an inherited prestige (*baka*) which was a qualification to be taken into account by the electors. The theory of *baka* is of course a close parallel to the emphasis in royal lineages on the superior merit of sons of royal mothers as well as of royal fathers.[1] In both cases a theory was developed to justify the inclination of office-holders to concentrate the transmission of office in their own descent lines and to exclude collaterals.

The genealogical data are too fragmentary to permit a complete reconstruction of the ties of descent and affinity among a single generation of office-holders in any one district of Negri Sembilan. But an incomplete illustration can be provided from Sungei Ujong by a review of what happened there during the nineteenth century. It has been explained[2] that Menangkabau influence was less strong in Sungei Ujong than elsewhere in Negri Sembilan and that the all-powerful *Waris* clan was divided into two sections, each headed by a chief of half the district. The Dato' Klana, who had the better historical title to be regarded as the chief of all Sungei Ujong, then controlled only the Waris di-Darat territory upstream on the River Linggi from the modern town of Seremban. The Dato' Bandar of Waris di-Ayer was chief of the downstream half of the district. Up to the end of the eighteenth century the group within the Waris di-Darat which monopolized the office of Dato' Klana preserved a system of patrilineal transmission of office. Early in the nineteenth century a dispute arose between Dato' Klana Bahi and a strong personality called Kawal. Kawal was a son of Dato' Bandar Megah and also through his mother a grandson of a former Dato' Klana Leha. He could not hope to succeed his father as Dato' Bandar because that office was transmitted within a matrilineal descent group. He contended therefore that the office of Dato' Klana should, contrary to precedent, be inherited within a matrilineal descent group also. It was settled, not without a struggle, that this should be so. Thereafter the families of Bahi and Kawal shared the office of Dato' Klana. This arrangement was formalized by treating the matrilineal descendants of Dato' Klana Leha as one segment (Perut Ulu) and those of Bahi as another segment (Perut Hilir). The names of these two segments indicate that they lived in two villages along the river.[3] In theory

---

[1] See above, pp. 55 and 59.   [2] See above, pp. 38 and 76.

[3] This persists to this day. *Perut Ulu* has its village at what is now Mile 9 on the road from Seremban to Jelebu. *Perut Hilir* is at Mile 8. *Perut Hilir* has become

the office of Dato' Klana was to alternate between the two segments. In practice the alternation was irregular and its observance depended on the balance of power at the time. It happened that a sister of Dato' Klana Bahi married an Arab called Syed Ahmad. The son of this marriage, Syed Abdul Rahman, was of course eligible to succeed as Klana because he was a member of Perut Hilir. His prospects were improved by the fact that he was also a relative (described by one source as 'second nephew') of the powerful Dato' Bandar Tunggal. Syed Abdul Rahman, after being the power behind the throne in the last years of the elderly Dato' Klana Sending, succeeded him as Dato' Klana in 1871. When Abdul Rahman died in 1879 the British had to use their influence to prevent the irregular appointment of one of his sons as the next Dato' Klana. The successor who was appointed proved to be mentally deficient and he was eventually deposed. In 1890 Dato' Klana Ma'amor was appointed while still a boy. He married a woman of Perut Hilir, from which his own successor must come.[1] Ma'amor's sisters married important chiefs and one of his daughters married a man of Waris di-Ayer (a grandson of a former Dato' Bandar) who became Dato' Bandar in 1937 largely by the influence of his father-in-law, Dato' Klana Ma'amor.

The genealogical table below shows the extent to which important offices were held within a relatively small group of matrilineal kinsmen. The office of Dato' Johan denoted the head of Perut Ulu. (See diagram on page 80.)

There were of course other cases of intermarriage between Perut Ulu and Perut Hilir besides the case of Dato' Klana Ma'amor.

OUTSIDERS IN THE RULING CLASS

As a general rule membership of the ruling class was determined strictly by descent. But this general proposition requires some qualification in detail.

It was particularly difficult for a man born into the subject class of a Malay State to rise to aristocratic status in the same State. Being locally born his origin was known and beyond question. Yet it could happen that a peasant became a chief in his own State. The only instances so far traced come from Pahang. The first was To' Gajah of Pulau Tawar who was the son of a Rawa (Sumatran) immigrant. He rose to become one of the most powerful chiefs in Pahang partly by his own remarkable ability,

[1] At the election of the Dato' Klana in 1946 after the death of Dato' Klana Ma'amor it was contended that one of his sons should succeed since he was both eligible and had a more illustrious pedigree (*baka*, see above, p. 78) than anyone else.

relatively numerous and has been further divided into *Kampong Manggis* and *Kampong Gedang*. At the election of the Dato' Klana in 1946 it was strenuously contended that *Kampong Manggis* and *Kampong Gedang* ought to take it in turn to provide the candidate of *Perut Hilir* when it was the turn of *Perut Hilir*.

WARIS DI-DARAT OF SUNGEI UJONG

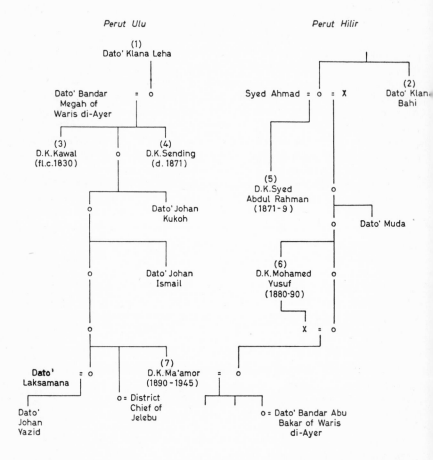

especially as a fighter, and partly by the Sultan's favour.[1] The other instance was the Orang Kaya of Semantan who had begun life as the Sultan's dog-boy and had risen by success in war and by the Sultan's favour.[2]

It is no accident that both these cases come from Pahang and no other State. Conditions in Pahang were primitive and turbulent. The Sultan

[1] *SSD*, 15 October 1887. His career is described in Linehan (1936); see especially p. 200.

[2] Clifford (*AR Phg*, 1890) gives this information of him. But it conflicts with Clifford's statement (*SSD*, 15 October 1888) that he was 'jealous of newly created chiefs'—an attitude which suggests that he was not of that category. See also Linehan op. cit., pp. 68 and 198.

had fought a civil war to establish his claim against his elder brother. Many of the chiefs were his enemies; it was natural that he should reward his supporters.

An *immigrant* adventurer could more easily win acceptance as a member of the ruling class. His claim to aristocratic status in his own country could not easily be checked. A Sumatran Syed in particular could always make a place for himself among the ruling class of a Malay State.[1] In addition to Syeds there were a number of Indonesian merchants and fighting men, especially Arab half-castes, Bugis (from the Celebes) and Achehnese (from North Sumatra) who ranked in the Malay States of the 1870 period as aristocrats.

There were considerable gradations of status within the ruling class of each state.[2] Many an aristocrat was a nobody despite his blue blood because he held no office and had no close kinsman or patron of standing. If such an 'aristocratic nobody' rose to wealth and power, he was considered an upstart by the established families despite his status as an aristocrat by birth. The outstanding example was Long Ja'afar, originally an unknown aristocrat in Perak, who became tax collector at Larut for his kinsman and patron, the Dato' Panglima Bukit Gantang. Long Ja'afar was remarkably successful in developing the tin mines of Larut and rose to be a district chief in his own right. His son, Ngah Ibrahim, attained in 1862 to the title of Mentri, one of the four chieftainships of the first class in Perak. Resentment against the Mentri gave rise to the story (quite untrue) that he was the son of an Indian/Malay half-caste trader from Province Wellesley.[3]

MALAY ARISTOCRATIC IDEAS OF STATUS

The idea of status ran through aristocratic Malay life in a dozen ways. Lesser members of the royal lineage sought to preserve their superior status as royalty by marrying wives of royal descent after the fashion of

[1] See pp. 79–80 for Syed Ahmad who married a sister of a Dato' Klana of Sungei Ujong and begot a son who became Dato' Klana. Another famous case was Syed Shaban, son of an Arab missionary of Malacca who married a daughter of the Yam Tuan Muda of Rembau (Negri Sembilan) and founded the royal lineage of Tampin. See also pp. 67, n. 2 and 93.

[2] Among other distinctions the amount of the bride-price varied; e.g. in Perak a mere 'man of position' married off his daughter for $62.50; a minor chief for $125; a major chief for $250; a Raja Muda for $500 and a Sultan for $1,000. Wilkinson (1908a), p. 15.

[3] Swettenham (1948), p. 123 hints at the story with 'The Mantri himself was not a pure Malay; he was partly Indian and the Indian blood gave him a shrewdness and business capacity foreign to Malays.' In the latter part of this sentence one can feel the sneer of Swettenham's aristocratic informant.

Wilkinson (1924) p. 78, gives the genealogy as it really was and states 'Long Ja'afar was not (as is usually believed) a shrewd trader from Penang or Province Wellesley, but a Perak-born Malay'.

the 'inner circle' of potential successors to the throne.[1] Among the non-royal members of the ruling class intermarriage with a commoner was disapproved.[2] Even in democratic Negri Sembilan marriage payments and other kindred matters were made the means of differentiating status.[3]

Differential status found verbal expression in many ways. There were innumerable proverbs on class distinctions and the impropriety of not observing them.[4] Members of the royal lineage bore the title 'Raja' or 'Tunku' and non-royal aristocrats could often lay claim to 'Dato' ' or 'Tuan'.[5] Peasants who addressed a member of the ruling class were expected to conform to certain rules of linguistic usage designed to emphasize their lowly status. Even in Negri Sembilan members of the lineages entitled to fill political offices could be described (but not addressed) by special terms.[6]

There were a number of general status terms in use. *Pangkat* denoted rank, position or status; it particularly denoted the status of holding office. A chief or other holder of a conferred title was described as *bergelar* (a man of title). *Taraf* was less often used to denote a level of social standing. In Negri Sembilan *kupu* was used in the context of marriage alliances to indicate that the families of the spouses were of equal status.

In the proverbs a connexion was traced between status by birth and good manners; e.g. *Usul menunjokkan asal*—manners reveal origin. One may compare the English usage of 'breeding'.

The material equipment of Malay society was equally a medium for the demonstration of status. Certain architectural features of houses; the use of yellow in clothing, curtains, hangings, etc.; the use of certain types of ornaments and weapons; the way in which articles of clothing and the Malay dagger were worn; the number of pillows on a wedding dais;[7] all these things differed according to the status of the individual.

It was a society dominated by the idea of comparative status. Such status was mainly ascribed by the fact of birth into a particular station. Within the high status group however distinctions were made between mere ascribed status and the achievement of power and prestige expressed in the conferment of a title (*gelaran*) or an office (*pangkat*); title and office usually went together. This possibility of achieving status introduced a certain spirit of competition into aristocratic life.

INTERMARRIAGE IN THE RULING CLASS

Marriage as a factor in the distribution of political power can be considered

[1] See above, pp. 59 and 67.   [2] See below, p. 86.

[3] See above, p. 75.   [4] See above, p. 65.

[5] See above, pp. 22 and 66.   [6] See above, p. 75.

[7] Significantly it was considered the major achievement of the reign of Sultan Mohamed Shah of Malacca that he instituted many of these rules. See Brown (1952), pp. 54–9. See also Skeat (1900), pp. 370–1 on the significance of pillows on a wedding dais.

in two aspects. There is first the aspect of transmission of authority from one generation to another: e.g. a Malay aristocrat in choosing a wife for himself or a husband for his daughter had an eye to the future status by birth of the children of such a union. Some examples of this aspect of the matter have already been given.[1] It will not be further pursued.

The second aspect of the subject is the creation of affinal ties as a means of concentrating and augmenting power and authority in the generation of the spouses. This aspect has been touched on in considering the other aspect, but only incidentally. A bond between members of the ruling class was much needed. Power was dispersed in the hands of district chiefs who vied with each other for prestige and advantage. The remainder of the ruling class was grouped in lineages around the holders of the chieftainships; each group, like the chief at its head, in opposition to others. There were elements in the situation, such as the Sultanate,[2] which tended to hold the ruling class together despite its organizational tendency to strife and fission. Intermarriage between members of different lineages was another and important factor tending to promote unity. The aristocrats themselves did not of course view their marriages as a means of preserving the unity of the State. They regarded each alliance from the standpoint of their own interest and advancement. By establishing affinal ties they obtained allies.

As a preliminary to a review of aristocratic marriage it is necessary to describe the relatively favourable position of the Malay women who were the partners of these unions. Malay women of the aristocratic class did not themselves exercise any appreciable political influence or power. They took no part in the political discussions of their husbands and fathers. They held no political office though a few held court titles. They were not members of any assembly in which political affairs were debated. Yet by their very existence they were a political factor—as personalities and as the media of affinal ties. Swettenham thus describes the position of a married Malay lady of the upper class:

> 'As the wife of an official she takes an interest in State affairs, and does her best to push her husband's claims to preferment and title; in this last ambition she has a special interest, for certain offices and titles held by the husband confer rank and title on his principal wife, and that helps greatly to assure her position. It is also the custom to grant offices, titles and salaries to ladies connected with the court, and in these cases, the husband, if there is one, is not concerned. Malay women of the better class, and most of those in the entourage of the Sultan and the leading Rajas, are distinctly intelligent if they cannot be called highly educated. They are usually of a cheerful temperament, capital company, witty and interesting, with a strong sense of humour; a man has to do his best to hold his own in their society.'[3]

[1] See above, pp. 55, 67, 78.

[2] See above, p. 49.

[3] Swettenham (1948), p. 155. Some of this description refers to the era of British protection rather than before but it seems a fair general picture of the Malay lady of 1870.

Malay women were greatly prized for their beauty and charm. The seduction of other men's wives was one of the main interests of gilded youth too young for political authority. Husbands therefore guarded their wives jealously but were criticized if they did not allow them the customary degree of personal liberty.

Muslim rules of purdah were ignored. Malay women did not wear the veil and they might appear in the presence of men other than their husbands and kinsfolk. They did not however take part in the entertainment of their husband's guests nor were they allowed to travel without the escort of a kinsman or a trusted servant. In and around their houses they had considerable freedom of movement—the more so as their husbands were frequently away from home on a journey or residing in another house. Semi-public occasions such as a wedding afforded an occasion for the display of their charms and their wit.

Married women of the ruling class often controlled substantial wealth. It was common to make a 'marriage settlement' in writing at the time of the wedding.[1] It is not recorded what was written into these settlements. Presumably the husband either made a gift of property to his wife or acknowledged that property brought into the marriage by the wife was hers and not his. It was also a general rule that 'the income of a woman from her own private property is independent of any control by her husband'.[2]

It was expected of the husband that he would provide a house for his wife as her property:

'It is customary among Malays of rank or position to appropriate a particular house to the use of his wife at the time of marriage. She is entitled to live there during coverture, and if she is divorced by the husband, the house is regarded as hers and is assigned to her for her use during her life.'[3]

If the husband had more than one wife he was expected to provide a house for each. At the husband's death it appears that his daughters had a better claim than his sons to inherit his houses.[4]

The wife of a chief or other wealthy aristocrat was the mistress of a numerous household. For in the event of a chief's or a Sultan's marriage it was customary to round up young women from the surrounding villages to serve as maids (*dayang*) and nurses (*inang* or *pengasoh*).[5] Some of these handmaidens were slave women or debtors.[6] Unless given in marriage by the master of the house, female servants were expected to remain unmarried and were punished if caught in unauthorized unchastity.[7] The

---

[1] Swettenham (1895), p. 9.   [2] *PSC*, 26 October 1882.

[3] *PSC*, 4 March 1879. But the husband would not assign to his wife his principal residence 'surrounded by extensive fortifications'.

[4] An inference from the dispositions of Long Ja'afar of Larut who left his principal house to his daughter and smaller houses to his widow and his son. *PSC*, 4 March 1879.

[5] Maxwell (1890).   [6] See below, pp. 97–105.

[7] See below, p. 103 on the question of enforced prostitution.

lady of the house kept her staff employed in domestic tasks such as cooking, sewing, sweeping, fetching water, etc.

Aristocratic women also had freedom to engage in business activities outside the limits of the household. There are instances from the 1870 period of Malay ladies who owned tin mines, who took trade goods on a journey to visit relatives and who bid for a contract to collect taxes.[1] In 1878 it was found that the two largest investors in debt-slaves in Perak were women.[2]

Wives were expected to be tolerant of their husbands' infidelities. It appears that there was usually no trouble provided that the rival was not under the same roof and that there was not an open scandal. There was much resentment if the husband took a second wife, as under Muslim law he was permitted to do. Swettenham says:

'I have often discussed the position of married women with the leaders of Malay society, and I have been struck by the fact that they have only one complaint to make, and that is their strong objection to being one wife of several.'[3]

It was not unusual to stipulate at the time of marriage that the wife should be entitled to a divorce if the husband subsequently took a second wife.[4]

This question of personal relations between spouses was of importance because the marriage was an expression of an alliance between their families. It could happen that friction between husband and wife led to a quarrel between husband and father-in-law.[5]

Nonetheless marriages were often made for dynastic reasons without much regard for personal compatibility.[6] The norm of approved conduct did not permit an unmarried girl of marriageable age to consort with young men. Her parents were criticized and her own matrimonial prospects were injured if she were not kept at home between puberty and marriage (Malay girls were married as young as fourteen). To be a gadabout (*bergaul*) was not approved. The rules did not however prevent the occurrence of clandestine affairs between young men and women (whether

[1] Che Mida and the tin mines—See *PSC*, 12 March 1882. See also Swettenham (1951), p. 47 on Che Mida's marriage with the Laxamana as a strictly business proposition. Che Ngah Nahra mentioned her journey with trade goods (tin going downstream and fish on the return trip) to *PCE*. Toh Puan Halimah bid for certain tax farms in Larut after the exile of her husband, the Mentri of Larut. *PSC*.

[2] Report by Hugh Low dated 14 December 1878. *Slavery Papers*, laid before Parliament.

[3] Swettenham (1948), p. 154.

[4] Winstedt (1947a), p. 38.

[5] One such case was the marriage of Tunku Kudin of Kedah to Tunku Chik, daughter of Sultan Abdul Samad of Selangor. The estrangement is mentioned in *SSD*, 26 October 1877.

[6] 'When the Malay States were entirely independent, it is probable that no girl was ever consulted as to her wishes in the matter of matrimony.' Swettenham (1948), p. 153. This of course was true only of a first marriage. A divorcee or widow had considerable freedom of choice.

maidens or wives).[1] The essential point is that even if a young man or woman succeeded in conceiving a passionate attachment, this fact was not necessarily or even frequently the making of a marriage.

Marriage was a serious business arranged by parents and other older kinsfolk. The main consideration was to marry within one's class:

> 'Malays are extremely particular about questions of rank and birth, especially when it comes to marriage, and *mésalliances*, as understood in the West, are with them rare.'[2]

There was thus a general practice of class endogamy which was enforced with particular strictness on the women.[3] Within the ruling class persons of royal descent in the male line tended to form an endogamous sub-group.[4] Except in Negri Sembilan there were no exogamous groups and, subject to the Islamic rules on 'prohibited degrees' of relationship for the purpose of marriage, anyone might marry whom he pleased. In particular there was no objection in Perak or Selangor to marriage between members of the same lineage. In Negri Sembilan the practice varied in particular cases but in general the exogamous unit was the lineage; marriage between members of the same clan but of different lineages was permissible. There was also a special Negri Sembilan rule against marriage of the children of two brothers.[5]

These rules allowed considerable room for manoeuvre in contracting politically advantageous unions. The information on this subject is incomplete because the extant patrilineal genealogies frequently omit to state the family of the mother. But there is enough data available to support the proposition that aristocratic marriage was a political alliance.

Some illustrations have already been given in previous sections of this paper. Thus Sultan Abdullah of Perak (1874–6) and Sultan Idris (1887–1916) had, while still aspirants to the throne, improved their prospects by marrying a daughter of their respective predecessors.[6] In Selangor the group which controlled the Sultanate and the important central districts of the state were united by affinal ties only.[7] The genealogy of the Dato' Klanas of *Waris di-Darat* of Sungei Ujong (Negri Sembilan) shows how Dato' Klana Ma'amor, following the practice of his predecessors, established a web of affinal ties through the marriage of himself and of his sisters to useful allies.[8]

---

[1] Swettenham gives this account of the situation at the royal capital of Selangor in 1874. 'The business of the place was piracy, its serious pleasure love-making—legitimate or otherwise, but mainly otherwise—and its lighter recreations gambling, opium-smoking and duelling. . . . The younger women resorted to weapons for the settlement of their quarrels and a girl would stab a rival or a faithless lover, as soon as not.' Swettenham (1895), p. 67.

[2] Swettenham (1895), p. 8.

[3] 'While a Malay Raja could marry a person of any rank, that liberty was not enjoyed by his women folk.' Winstedt (1947a), p. 41.

[4] See above, p. 67.   [5] Winstedt, op. cit., p. 37.   [6] See above, p. 57.

[7] See above, pp. 57 and 72.   [8] See above, p. 80.

The case of Ngah Ibrahim, Mentri of Larut, provides a further example of marriage as a form of political alliance.

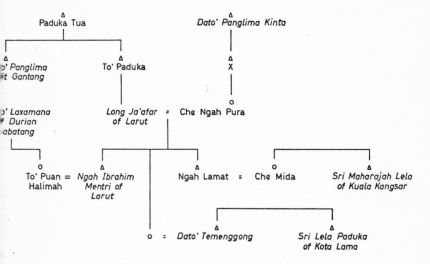

(Italics indicate a district chief)

It will be seen that Ngah Ibrahim inherited the district of Larut (and with it the greatest wealth in Perak) from his father. He was a great-nephew on his father's side of the Dato, Panglima Bukit Gantang; he was a son-in-law of the Dato' Laxamana of Durian Sabatang; through his mother he was a great-grandson of the Dato' Panglima Kinta; through his brother he was a brother-in-law of the Sri Maharaja Lela of Kuala Kangsar; through his sister he was a brother-in-law of the Dato' Temenggong and of the Sri Lela Paduka of Kota Lama. The table above is merely a selection of affinal ties viewed from the Mentri of Larut as the centre-point. The various families were related in other ways as well. For example Che Mida, after the death of Ngah Lamat, contracted a brief marriage with the Dato' Laxamana, thus becoming the mother-in-law of her late husband's brother.

The table shows the ties resulting from intermarriage over more than one generation. Ngah Ibrahim was related to the family of the Dato' Panglima Bukit Gantang through his father.[1] He was related to the family of the Dato' Panglima Kinta because of the marriage alliance contracted

[1] Long Ja'afar's brother (not shown in the table) had married a daughter of the Dato' Panglima Bukit Gantang. There was thus an affinal tie and a descent tie between the same groups (Wilkinson (1924), p. 78). The information used in the table has been gleaned from many sources and there are occasional variances; e.g. it is not entirely certain that Long Ja'afar was a nephew of the Dato' Panglima Bukit Gantang (see however Swettenham (1951), p. 47.)

by his father. It is only with the alliances of Ngah Ibrahim and his contemporaries that ties are made, as distinct from inherited. The marriage
alliances of this second generation would of course give rise to the descent
ties of the next generation. Since the circle of eligible spouses was
relatively limited, there was a tendency for everybody to be related
to everybody else through several lines. It was however the immediate affinal links which seem to have been politically significant above all
others.

To illustrate the significance of these affinal ties it is necessary to
review the course of politics and warfare in each State to see how political
alliances coincided with matrimonial ties. The coalition of affinal kinsmen
around the Sultan of Selangor has been mentioned more than once.[1] The
case of the Mentri of Larut, just illustrated as an example of affinal ties,
can be further analysed in terms of political coalitions. In the mid-nineteenth century Perak was virtually divided into two parts by the hostility
of opposed coalitions of chiefs. The Mentri of Larut was the wealthiest
and ablest of the chiefs of 'Up-River' (*Ulu*) Perak. The families of Kinta
and Bukit Gantang, with which he was connected, were by tradition the
leading potentates of the eastern and western flanks of the Up-River
area. Kuala Kangsar and Kota Lama were important strong-points on the
upper reaches of the Perak River itself. The Dato' Laxamana of Durian
Sabatang however was a leader of the 'Down-River' (*Hilir*) group. In
marrying the daughter of the Dato' Laxamana, the Mentri of Larut was
bridging a barrier of hostility.[2]

In 1873 the Mentri of Larut was in difficulty owing to civil war among
the Chinese miners in his district of Larut. He appealed for help to Sultan
Ismail, who owed his position as Sultan to the support of the Up-River
coalition and who was related to the Mentri through the Kinta family.
Sultan Ismail sent two envoys; these were (1) their common kinsman,
the Dato' Panglima Kinta, and (2) the chief of Kuala Kangsar, the Mentri's
nephew. Meanwhile the Mentri obtained reinforcements of eighty armed
men from the Dato' Temenggong, who was his brother-in-law. The
trouble in Larut had been fomented by the Down-River faction but it is
remarkable that the Dato' Laxamana, a leading member of that faction
and an arch-intriguer, took no part in weakening the position of the
Mentri, who was his son-in-law.

The examples have generally been of alliances between individuals of
equal standing. There was another, very common form of matrimonial/
political alliance when a man of aristocratic birth but without resources
of his own married the daughter of a chief whom he hoped to make his
patron. This was a case of the weak attaching themselves to the strong.
But it was an attachment of mutual interest. The bridegroom might hope

---

[1] See above, pp. 58 and 72.

[2] Much as medieval kings of England and other European countries sometimes
married the daughters of their arch-enemies.

to be given a village to administer or taxes to collect. The chief obtained an adherent upon whose loyalty he could rely.

To sum up, the ruling class was a group perpetuating itself by the rule that membership depended on descent from a former member of the group. It was organized into a number of lineages, each associated with control of a district exercised by a district chief drawn from the lineage and assisted by other members of that lineage. The ruling class was a community in which there was keen competition within each lineage for office and the fruits of office and between lineages for greater territory, wealth and power at the expense of others. Affinal ties were of some importance in cementing political alliances between chiefs and generally in holding the ruling class together. Swettenham's picture of the situation is:

'Amongst the higher classes everyone knows everyone else, and relationships are recognized to what seems remote kinship. The clan feeling is universal, and an insult or injury to a relative, friend or follower of a powerful chief is strongly resented and may in a moment, lead to very serious consequences.'[1]

It was not a community organized purely on lines of descent but rather of descent supplemented by ties of locality. The state itself was a unit of territory symbolized in the Sultan and the royal lineage descended from the Sultans of Malacca or some other illustrious origin. The remainder of the ruling class of each state however was merely an aggregate of unrelated lineages (in their first origin) grouped by the fact of common residence and pre-eminence within the territory of the State. Each lineage was itself a territorial as well as a descent group by virtue of its association with a particular district.

A Note on the individual Chieftainships of Perak, Selangor and Negri Sembilan

It is most necessary to distinguish between the theory and the practice of Malay chieftainships of this period. There were titles borne by chiefs which had been conferred by Sultans of Malacca on those of their officers who performed particular functions in the government of the city state of Malacca. The Temenggong was the commander of the troops and of the police; the Laxamana was the admiral—and so on. In the nineteenth century some of these titles had been acquired by chiefs of districts who performed none of the traditional functions of the office. Many others existed in theory only; the offices themselves were vacant.

In a review of the chieftainships it is essential to ignore the traditional Malacca functions of each office. It has also to be stressed that there were far fewer actual chiefs than the theory of the constitution supposed. The theory was elaborate and well-remembered—as part of the Malacca tradition—e.g. refer to the account of the Perak chieftainships at pp. 134–58 of Wilkinson and Winstedt's *History of Perak*.[2] There were

[1] Swettenham (1900), p. 142.

[2] Wilkinson and Winstedt (1934).

G

supposed to be four chiefs of the first rank, eight of the second, sixteen of the third and even thirty-two of the fourth. In practice there were were about a dozen chiefs in all.

The Perak tradition illustrates the preoccupation of Malay political theory with multiples of four. The theory demanded multiples of four and the memory of offices long defunct was kept alive to make up the required number.

PERAK

The position in 1874, so far as the fragmentary evidence goes, was as follows:

The Four Chiefs

(1) The office of *Bendahara* had since the late eighteenth century been appropriated by the royal family to make a third royal office (the other two being Sultan and Raja Muda) to fit the tripartite division of the royal dynasty and the connected rules of rotation which evolved at about the same time. See pp. 56–7 and 72.

(2) The office of *Temenggong* was held by the district chief of Kota Lama near Kuala Kangsar in upstream Perak.

(3) The office of *Orang Kaya Besar* was in abeyance.

(4) The office of *Mentri* was held by the district chief of Larut.

The Eight Chiefs

(1) The office of *Maharaja Lela* was held by the district chief of Pasir Salak midway between upstream and downstream Perak.

(2) The office of *Laxamana* was held by the district chief of Durian Sabatang. He was the leader of the downstream confederacy of chiefs and controlled the mining district of Batang Padang.

(3) The office of *Sri Adika Raja* was vacant in 1874. It was usually held by a member of a lineage dominant in the furthest upstream district of Perak and was associated with control of that area.

(4) The office of *Shahbandar* was held by the district chief of Bandar, the port at the mouth of the Perak River. To some extent Bandar was the royal town in downstream Perak and the Dato' Shahbandar, in addition to collecting those customs revenues which were his own perquisite assisted the Sultan in the collection of royal revenues.

(5) The office of *Panglima Kinta* was held by the district chief of Kinta in east central Perak. It was to some extent an office of warden of the eastern frontier; items (2), (3) and (6) being wardens of the north, the south and the west.

(6) The office of *Panglima Bukit Gantang* had been vacant since 1871 though a son of the late chief was the recognized heir and attempted to exercise some of the functions of district chief. The office remained

vacant until revived in modern times. Its decline was the result of the rise of the neighbouring district chief of Larut (see item (4) of the Four Chiefs). As the chiefs of Larut rose to power the older dynasty of Bukit Gantang (the pass between the valley of the Perak River and Larut itself) fell into obscurity.

(7) The office of *Sri Agar di-Raja* ('*Sagor*' for short) was held by the district chief of Kampong Gajah in the upper reaches of downstream Perak.

(8) *Imam Paduka Tuan* was a religious office. It is uncertain whether this office was filled in 1874. It was not associated with the control of any particular district.

There is no certain list of the sixteen and the thirty-two chiefs of the third and fourth rank. Those offices which are known to have existed were not generally held by district chiefs but rather by their assistants, successors designate, etc.

SELANGOR

Braddell[1] mentions some non-royal chieftainships of Selangor. These were the offices of Penggawa Permatang, Penggawa Tua, Penghulu Aru and Orang Kaya Kechil and it appears that in origin they had been district chieftainships. However that may be, they seem to have been in abeyance in 1874. No holder of any such office had control of any district. There is no mention of them anywhere except in the memorandum by Braddell cited above.

The population of Selangor was so small that it could not support a ruling class beyond the various branches of the royal (Bugis-Rhio) dynasty. Members of this dynasty took over the district chieftainships. There were no royal titles for such offices and they disdained, as princes, to use the titles of non-royal chiefs. The position in the five valleys of Selangor was as follows:

(1) *Bernam* had for at least two or three generations past been controlled by a separate branch of the royal lineage the exact origin of which has not been traced. The chief of the 1870 period was through his mother a nephew of Sultan Abdul Samad, i.e. his father had married the Sultan's sister.

(2) *Selangor* was the original royal district of Selangor though the Sultans had ceased to live there by the middle of the nineteenth century. Up to 1870 the Selangor district was administered by the Sultan's eldest son and heir, Raja Muda Musa. It then changed hands in the course of the civil war.

(3) *Klang* was the royal capital of Selangor and the Klang valley was the royal district until 1866 when Sultan Abdul Samad withdrew from Klang at the outbreak of the civil war. During the reign of the previous

[1] *SSD*, 24 February 1874.

Sultan the Klang district had been managed by his son, Raja Sulaiman. On Sulaiman's death the old Sultan passed over Sulaiman's son, Raja Mahdi, and gave the district to his son-in-law, Raja Abdullah. He was no doubt persuaded to do so by Raja Juma'at, brother of Raja Abdullah and also son-in-law to the Sultan; Raja Juma'at was the power behind the throne. Klang became the bone of contention in the civil war (1866–73) between the heirs and allies of Raja Abdullah and a coalition headed by Raja Mahdi. From about 1870 onwards it was the district assigned by the Sultan (Abdul Samad) to his son-in-law, Tunku Kudin, whom he had appointed 'Viceroy' of all Selangor.

(4) *Langat* was a less important district than the others. It was at the disposition of the Sultan—in so far as he dared dispose of it. In 1867 Sultan Abdul Samad gave Langat to his son-in-law, Tunku Kudin of Kedah. Soon afterwards there was an exchange whereby the Sultan took over Langat and gave Klang to Kudin—if he could hold it.

(5) *Lukut* was the richest mining district of Selangor in the middle of the nineteenth century though it had declined in importance by 1870 because the deposits had been worked out. Lukut was granted to Raja Juma'at in 1846 by Sultan Mohamed for services rendered. On Juma'at's death in 1864 his son, Raja Bot, succeeded him. In 1846 Juma'at was a nephew of the consort of the reigning Sultan; soon afterwards he married a daughter of the Sultan. Lukut was ceded to Negri Sembilan in a frontier adjustment of 1880.

In conclusion it must be said that there were a few titles of office but they do not seem to have been associated with particular districts. Raja Juma'at apparently bore the title of 'Raja Tua' to indicate his seniority over all other members of the royal lineage (except of course the Sultan). This title may have lapsed at Juma'at's death in 1864. Abdul Samad bore the title 'Tunku Panglima Besar' during the reign of Sultan Mohamed, whose nephew and son-in-law he was. When Abdul Samad became Sultan, the title of 'Tunku Panglima Besar' was conferred on Raja Saman (or Berkat), a kinsman and brother-in-law of the new Sultan. In so far as the title indicated any duties it implied that the holder was the Sultan's adviser and executive assistant (a sort of Malay equivalent of the American 'Presidential aide').

Among non-royal leaders, there are incidental references to Dato' Shahbandar Yaseh who seems at one time to have had a stockade at Kuala Lumpur, inland up the Klang valley. The leader of the Javanese immigrants was the Dato' Dagang, whose interest extended from Kuala Langat to Kuala Lumpur. The leader of the Mandiling (Sumatran) immigrants was one Sutan Puasa, whose stronghold was at Kajang on the upper reaches of the Langat. He also had a part in the development of Kuala Lumpur.

NEGRI SEMBILAN

The words 'Negri Sembilan' mean 'Nine States' but it is agreed that the title has never connoted nine specific districts.

By tradition there have long been four major districts of Negri Sembilan each ruled by a chief with the title of 'Undang'. In historic times these four districts were Sungei Ujong, Rembau, Jelebu and Johol. There were also some minor semi-independent district chiefs attached to certain of these major districts.

(1) *Sungei Ujong* was in the nineteenth century virtually divided in two. The Undang (whose title was 'Dato' Klana') retained the inland area. The Dato' Shahbandar was the independent ruler of the middle reaches of the Linggi River, including the important tin-mines of Rasah.

(2) *Linggi* was a small district carved out of Sungei Ujong at the mouth of the Linggi River. Its people were Bugis who, according to tradition, were driven out of Rembau because they refused to conform to the alien matrilineal social system of Rembau. This episode occurred at the beginning of the nineteenth century and was probably the last flicker of the long-drawn wars between Bugis and Sumatran peoples in and around the coastal fringe of Negri Sembilan. The chief of Linggi bore the title 'Dato' Muda Linggi'. Until the twentieth century the title descended in the male line. The Dato' Muda Linggi is regarded as a nominal vassal of the Dato' Klana of Sungei Ujong.

(3) *Sungai Raya* and *Lukut* on the coast of what is now Negri Sembilan were until the frontier rectification of 1880 part of Selangor. They had been established by the Bugis invaders of the eighteenth century.

(4) *Rembau* had but one district chief, the Undang. But the right to fill this office alternated between two clans (see p. 77). Succession disputes occasioned fighting. In the 1880's there were for a time two rival claimants to the office.

(5) *Tampin* was a district carved out of Rembau during the first half of the nineteenth century by a branch of the royal lineage of Negri Sembilan. The district chief was called the 'Tunku Besar Tampin'.

(6) *Inas* and *Gemencheh* were two minor districts settled by later immigrants and carved out of *Johol*. The Dato' Inas and the Dato' Gemencheh acknowledged the Undang of Johol as their superior chief.

(7) *Jelebu* had but one district chief (Undang). A branch of the royal lineage had however established itself in Jelebu and its head bore the title 'Yam Tuan Muda Jelebu'. The royal intruders were driven out towards the end of the nineteenth century.

In addition to these more or less independent districts there was an inner block of four minor districts around the royal capital at *Sri Menanti*. These districts were recognized as the royal domain (*Tanah Mengandong*

Yam Tuan). Their chiefs were subject to rather more direct control by the Yam Tuan. Each chief bore the title *Dato'* followed by the name of his district, i.e. *Terachi, Ulu Muar, Jempol* and *Gunong Pasir*.

Within each district of Negri Sembilan the clan head of each matrilineal clan bore a title, e.g. the Dato' Andalika Mandulika of *Waris di-Darat*, Sungei Ujong.

The royal family had a number of lesser titles such as Tunku Besar, Tunku Laxamana and Tunku Panglima Perang. But these titles did not indicate chieftainship of districts.

5

The Chief in his District

Preceding chapters have described the rulers and the ruled. It has been necessary to mention incidentally some aspects of the political system as a method of control. This and the next two chapters deal primarily with political leadership as a function performed by the ruling class in relation to the subject class.

THE SULTANATE

It has been explained that the Sultans did not usually exercise strong authority over the ruling class of their States.[1] There was however one significant exception to this proposition. The Sultan of Pahang was a powerful ruler and much feared by his chiefs. This situation was in part a result of the result of a civil war in which the Sultan had fought his way to power and had incidentally defeated many leading chiefs.[2] It may also be explained by the fact that in Pahang at this time there was comparatively little tin-mining. The greater part of the revenues of the State were collected as import duties on goods entering by way of the royal capital at the mouth of the Pahang River. The total revenues of Pahang were less than those of the western States but the Sultan received a larger share of them. Wealth was the basis of power because it provided the means to attract a following.

Apart from his ritual functions[3] and his rarely exercised powers in the field of external relations[4] and national defence, the Sultan was little more in terms of power than a district chief in control of the district appropriated to him. Much of what follows on the subject of district chiefs applies equally to the Sultan in his royal domain.

THE DISTRICT CHIEF

The key institution in the political system was the district chief. He had control of an area, generally a side valley or a stretch of the valley of the main river of the State, and of all the people in it. The chief was appointed to his office by the Sultan by the issue of a letter of appointment and by

[1] See above, pp. 44–9.

[2] See Linehan (1936), pp. 66–89.

[3] See above, pp. 45–7.

[4] See above, p. 49.

the gift of a sword as the symbol of his office.[1] There is some conflict as to the practice over letters of appointment. It is asserted that it was 'the custom of all parts of the Peninsula' that a chief should hold a letter of appointment[2] but it was also said that 'few of the chiefs hold any authority from the sovereign for their occupation'.[3] This is no doubt a familiar case of divergent norm and actual practice. Where letters were issued there was no set form.[4] The district granted had to be named but not defined in detail by its boundaries on all sides.[5] The rights and privileges arising from the grant were usually left to be implied by well-known custom.[6] The grant of a district gave authority to govern and to collect taxes. In

[1] On the symbolic significance of weapons, see below, p. 123.

[2] Clifford, *SSD*, 28 April 1887.

[3] Braddell, *SSD*, 31 January 1879.

[4] The official translation of a grant of the district of Lukut in Selangor reads as follows:

'In the year 1262 on the 10th day of the month of Shaban (4 August 1846) at this time a document was made by His Majesty the Yang di-Pertuan Besar of Selangor in the country of Malacca bestowing to Raja Juma'at ibni Raja Ja'afar of Rhio the country of Lukut as far as Kuala Linggi for ever that Lukut is under the government of our son, Raja Juma'at, the same is to descend to the children and grandchildren of Raja Juma'at. It became the gift of us the Yang di-Pertuan that our heirs and successors are not to claim it hereafter because it is thus in truth and in fact we have affixed our chop (sc: seal) to this paper.'

SSD, 2 August 1878. The grant is unusual in that the Sultan made it in Malacca (British territory) as part of a bargain by which Raja Juma'at took over responsibility to the Sultan's creditors in Malacca for very large debts. The creditors would otherwise have arrested the Sultan for debt. The grant in perpetuity to the heirs of the grantee was unusual and was later held to be *ultra vires*. By custom a Sultan could grant a district only for the life of himself and of the grantee. When the Sultan died his successor could in theory revoke the grant; when the chief died, his heir succeeded only if appointed in his own right by the Sultan.

On the history of the Lukut grant see Gullick (1953a), pp. 87 and 98. For an example of a district not re-granted to the son of a deceased chief see the case of Raja Mahdi of Klang mentioned at p. 72 above.

[5] The Lukut grant quoted above refers to 'the country of Lukut as far as Kuala Linggi'. This definition meant the basin of the Lukut River and an extension along the coast as far as the mouth of the next river, the Linggi. In general it was sufficient to name the river in order to grant the whole area of the river basin. A grant cited in Linehan (1936), p. 213 includes:

'. . . confers upon Wan Daud ibni Wan Pahang the title of Maharaja Setia Raja with jurisdiction over the River Lipis from its mouth up to the point where the waters trickle down (to form a stream).'

[6] The grant quoted by Linehan (op. cit., see n. 5 above) defines the relations between two chiefs resident in the same valley and goes on:

'Now all the people in Lipis must observe and obey the instructions of those two Chiefs provided they are in accord with custom and the law of God. Whoever refuses to observe and obey the instructions of those two Chiefs shall be guilty of treason towards His Highness the Sultan and of an offence against Us, and We shall inflict the severest punishment upon them; confiscation or, in case of resistance, death.'

consideration of making the grant the Sultan could demand either a lump sum gift at the time or a share of the revenues of the district.[1]

As has been explained[2] the selection of a chief was largely determined by the claims of the lineage which customarily provided the holder of that office. Unless the Sultan was very powerful or the lineage very weak, the Sultan recognized that the lineage which was in control of the district must be allowed to provide the next chief as it had provided the last. A chief was often the son and almost always a patrilineal kinsman of his predecessor.

A chief held his district by his own strength rather than by the backing of the Sultan. It is therefore necessary at this point to consider the subject of a chief's 'following' and the related question of 'debt-bondage'. The power of a chief rested on the size of his following.

THE CHIEF'S FOLLOWING

A chief had an entourage of sons, brothers, sons-in-law, remoter kinsmen and other *aristocratic* supporters who acted as deputies and lieutenants in the work of government and performed the duties of secretary, comptroller of the household, mine-manager, captain-at-arms, envoy and confidant as occasion required. The size of this retinue varied with the wealth and standing of the chief. The significant aspect of this group was that its members were of the ruling class like their patron.

A chief and indeed any member of the ruling class who had a regular income also had a following of the peasant or subject class. These followers were known as *kawan*.[3] They included (1) volunteers and free mercenaries (2) debt-bondsmen and (3) female followers who were usually in bondage. Slaves and debt-bondsmen were often treated as a single class but strictly a slave was not a 'follower' because that term implied the status of a free man.[4] Debt-bondage and slavery are discussed later.[5]

A chief's following served certain utilitarian purposes and it was also an index of prestige. The males were generally young men and their profession was fighting. There were also secretaries (of the humbler type), boatmen and servants of various kinds. The male followers were the

---

[1] In the Lukut grant (see p. 96, n. 4 above) Raja Juma'at took over the Sultan's debts to the amount of $169,000 (£35,000) but this was exceptional. The Sultan of Pahang once demanded $1,000 and found no takers (*SSD*, 28 April 1887). As an example of revenue-sharing the Sultan of Selangor expected an annual tribute of money, rice and opium from the chief of Klang (*SSD*, 18 June 1878) and the Sultan of Perak was entitled to $6 per *bahara* (400 lb) on all tin exported from any district in Perak (*SSD*, 26 April 1875).

[2] See above, p. 70.

[3] This term could also be applied to aristocratic followers though the word *panakawan* was more correct in their case. Wilkinson (1932).

[4] The point is discussed at p. 104.　　　　　　[5] See below, p. 98ff.

bodyguard and striking force of the chief. They manned the stockade from which he controlled his district. They accompanied him on his journeys.[1]

The women were also young. They were the domestic servants of the chief's household and the mistresses and the potential wives of his male followers. Their position is discussed in connexion with the sexual aspects of debt-bondage.[2]

The followers depended on the chief for their keep.[3] Their prospects of obtaining 'pickings' depended on his wealth and power. A chief who was poor and powerless could not attract or retain a large following. On the other hand a chief with only a small following was likely to be ousted from his district by a rival with more men at his back. The size of a chief's following was thus the index of his power and status. Two European observers of this period commented that:

> 'The Raja looks to the number of his following as the gauge of his power and other Rajas will respect and fear him accordingly. Thus he tries to get men into his service in this way.' (i.e. as debtors.)[4]

> 'The ownership of a number of slaves and debt-bondsmen was the mark of a man of rank, wealth and influence.'[5]

From incidental references in the records it appears that a personal escort of 30–80 men was usual in the case of a chief of consequence. To travel with more than 100 men (unless several chiefs had joined forces) was considered aggressive towards those whose territory the party traversed. It was an attempt to overawe by a display of force. On the other hand to pay a visit with only three or four followers, and these unarmed, was a gesture of conciliation.[6]

Since followers were so often debt-bondsmen it is convenient to pass on to the subject of debt-bondage and slavery at this point.

DEBT-BONDAGE AND SLAVERY

Debt-bondage was a useful means of recruitment of followers since debtors, unlike mercenaries and free volunteers, could not desert their master at will. A debt-bondsman was *orang berhutang* and a slave was *abdi* or *hamba*.

---

[1] It was essential for prestige purposes to travel with a following of suitable size. For example, see Gullick (1953b), p. 81.

[2] See below, p. 103.

[3] In Pahang in 1889 it was estimated that followers cost about $4 p.m. each. Most of this expense was on food; clothing and opium were other items. *SSD*, 17 January 1890.

[4] Swettenham, *SSD*, 16 October 1875.   [5] Maxwell (1890).

[6] Thus a Malay chief in Perak who had long been hostile to the British protectorate regime paid a visit to two British administrators in this fashion. It was construed as an indication of his wish to bury the hatchet. *SSD*, 6 March 1879.

The European administrators who went into the Malay States in 1874 wrote many reports on 'debt-slavery'.[1] Slavery (in which they included debt-bondage) was a subject on which they and public opinion in the United Kingdom held strong views. The reports were thus written with a prejudice towards the subject-matter. The writers of the reports tended to generalize and to state as facts the stories told them by runaway bondsmen who had taken refuge with them and who had an interest in exaggerating their wrongs. Reports based on such data are not likely to be balanced and reliable. On the other hand after the revolt of 1875 known as the Perak War there was a more cautious and objective attitude to the subject since mishandling of the 'debt-bondage' question had been one of the causes of that revolt.

The best general account of debt-bondage is given by Swettenham. After explaining that chiefs did not permit their subjects to accumulate wealth he goes on:

'Thus when a *rayat* (or subject) is in want of money he goes to his *Raja* or chief to lend it him, because he alone can do so. Either money or goods are then lent, and a certain time stipulated for payment. If at the expiry of that time the money is not paid, it is usual to wait some time longer, say two or three or even six months. Should payment not then be made, the debtor, if a single man, is taken into the creditor's house; he becomes one of his followers and is bound to execute any order and do any work the Raja as creditor may demand, until the debt is paid, however long a time that may be. During this time the Raja usually provides the debtor with food and clothing, but if the creditor gives him money, that money is added to the debt. Often, however, the Raja gives nothing and the debtor has to find food and clothing as he can. Should the debtor marry—and the Raja will in all probability find him a wife—the wife and descendants are equally in debt bondage.'

'If, however, a large family were in bondage for the debt, one whose numbers seemed to the Raja to add to his dignity, then he would probably refuse to accept payment, not absolutely, but would say "Wait", and the waiting might last for years.'[2]

The debtor's work and services did not count towards reduction of the debt. Moreover the right of redemption was only nominal.

It is clear from this passage that debt-bondage, although in form an economic institution, was in substance a very mixed complex of several elements. The chief acquired and retained bondsmen as a means of augmenting his power and prestige. The bondsman might expect the creditor to provide him with a wife; the children of this union inherited the debtor status of the parent. The debtor's services, although considered to have some economic value, did not count towards the reduction

[1] A series of reports on debt-slavery were written in 1875 and were sent to the Colonial Office under cover of *SSD*, 16 October 1875. They were published with other papers relating to the Malay States in a Parliamentary Paper of 1875. They were republished as a separate Parliamentary Paper in 1882 and later reports written in the 1880's were published in a further Parliamentary Paper

[2] *SSD*, 16 October 1875.

of the debt. The debtor was usually a dependent of the creditor. Single men became followers, but not married men.

Debt-bondage was particularly significant in terms of the social relationship between the parties. This fact appears particularly in the information given about the transfer of debtors from one creditor to another and about the emancipation of debtors during the period of British protection. The rule was that a debtor could demand to be transferred to any other creditor who would pay off his debt to the original creditor. In practice transfers at the instance of the debtor were rare. Transfers at the instance of the creditor were common. Swettenham says:

'Moreover it was very common for a creditor to sell his debt-slaves when he was tired of them or wanted money, *and the bondspeople not infrequently suffered by the transfer.*'[1]

Transfer broke the personal tie which had grown out of the economic relationship. A Malay still living who can remember the last days of debt-bondage in Pahang has written:

'Some of the older ones had become really attached to their masters and regarded themselves as part of the family establishments.'[2]

Hugh Clifford noted that:

'There is no special hardship in this (bondage) as the children grow up as dependents on the sons of the house and are fed and clothed, and as a rule are kindly treated by their masters.'[3]

Finally there is Hugh Low's report on the reaction of creditors to a scheme in 1883 for emancipation of debtors by payment of their debts from government funds:

'How can we take money for our friends who have so long lived with us, many of them born in our houses? We can sell cattle, fruit or rice, but not take money for our friends.'[4]

This idyllic picture is not to be accepted without reservation. The early reports contain instances of ill-treatment of debtors supported by the personal knowledge of the reporting officer. When one human being is at the mercy of another, there will always be abuses of power. The question is not whether there were ever cases of ill-treatment but whether such cases were typical. One has general statements such as:

'The creditor did what he liked with his debt-slaves, and when they found life intolerable and ran away, if caught they were killed and no one objected, because anyone of position had debt-slaves of their own.'[5]

and others such as:

'Cases of ill-treatment of a debt-bondsman by a creditor are rare and the debt-bondsman has exactly the same redress that any other person would have.'[6]

[1] Swettenham (1948), p. 196. My italics.

[2] Dato' Sir Mahmud bin Mat, K.B.E., C.M.G. (1954), p. 10.

[3] *SSD*, 15 October 1887.   [4] *SSD*, 3 May 1883.   [5] Swettenham (1948), p. 195.

[6] W. G. Maxwell in *AR Kedah*, 1909. Note that this comment refers to a different State and a different period.

'No case of cruelty or any great hardship has been brought to my notice since I came into the country.'[1]

On balance it seems fair to conclude that the ruling class treated their bondsmen and slaves fairly. The vice of the system was that the bondsmen and slaves were inferior beings, almost chattels.

The economic aspect of debt-bondage, although it was not perhaps the most significant facet of the institution, deserves consideration. Here a distinction must be made between bondsmen who were and those who were not members of the household and personal following of the creditor.

Debt-bondsmen who were followers of their creditor were indeed an investment which could be realized by sale.[2] They were thus of economic value as capital. But from the standpoint of income and expenditure they cost more to keep than their services were worth. The nature of their relationship with the creditor as 'hangers on' precluded the possibility of their being given regular employment. If they had been assigned tasks, they would not have been available at beck and call. Long periods of idleness inevitably beget demoralization:

'Debtor servants, especially men as might be expected, are indolent and improvident and the worst of . . . labourers. In a few cases the women, as household servants, may be useful. . . . These people are inclined to theft, and their idle habits lead them into companionship of desperate men, which ends in robbery.'[3]

Swettenham noted that among debt-bondsmen 'gambling becomes a mania'[4] and elsewhere relates how on leaving an aristocratic household one morning he could not get anyone to carry his baggage down to the boat because 'all Che Mida's people were overcome by the effect of opium smoked the night before'.[5]

The question of the economic value of followers who were debtors came to a head when British administrators suggested that debt-bondage should be gradually abolished by counting the presumed value of the debtors' services against their debts. Malay chiefs in Perak replied that the services of their bondsmen had a value 'which was scarcely more than nominal'.[6]

[1] Hugh Low in a report dated 14 December 1878 in the slavery papers. Low did not come to the Malay States until they had been under British control for three years.

[2] Maxwell (1890) says that a chief might have 'several thousand dollars' invested in loans to bondsmen. Low (slavery report of 14 December 1878) says that debt-bondage was 'a favourite form of security'.

[3] This passage was written by Captain James Low with reference to Province Wellesley about 1830–40. It is quoted in *AR Kedah* 1909 as apt to conditions in Kedah at that time. There is no reason to think that it did not equally apply to Perak c. 1870.

[4] *SSD*, 16 October 1875. [5] Swettenham (1951), p. 78.

[6] Hugh Low in slavery report dated 14 December 1878.

Debt-bondsmen not in the personal following of their creditors were generally married men with families. They were put to agricultural work to produce food for the sustenance of their creditor and his household.[1] They thus contributed to providing the surplus with which to maintain a section of the community in a non-productive military and political role.

The most detailed account of the work of agricultural debt-bondsmen relates to Kedah when it came under British protection in 1909.[2] There were three types of work—(1) *kerja panjang pendek*, odd jobs of personal and domestic service; (2) *kerja dalam bendang*, cultivation in the rice fields; and (3) *kerja dalam dusun*, care of orchards. This last type of work was regarded as nominal and did not entitle the debtor to receive food and clothing from the creditor. Of Perak in the 1870's it was said that the work of a bondsman was 'every species of household drudgery, in clearing ground, and in raising padi and other articles of food'.[3] Another observer said of a chief's bondsmen in Perak that 'they served in his household, cultivated his fields and worked his mines.'[4]

The services of an agricultural bondsman relieved a chief of the necessity of cultivating the food which he ate and of doing domestic chores of one kind and another. He thus had leisure for military and political pursuits. There was no attempt, with the exception of some small ventures in tin-mining, to organize bondsmen for production on a large or industrial scale so as to obtain a surplus for sale. The explanation of this fact lies in the absence of market outlets for large quantities of produce and the lack of managerial staff for the organization of large-scale enterprises of this kind.[5]

The assignment of agricultural labour to people of low status had the inevitable consequence that no one of aristocratic birth would willingly demean himself to do such work.

A chief's following included a number of women who were for the most part either bondswomen or slaves. Some had been purchased or born into bondage. Others had been rounded up from the villages of the district under the custom which permitted a chief to recruit women as concubines or domestic servants in this way. To judge from the records

[1] Dato' Mahmud bin Mat (1954).

[2] Sir George Maxwell in *AR Kedah*, 1909.

[3] J. W. W. Birch, *SSD*, 16 October 1875.

[4] W. E. Maxwell (1890).

[5] Dato' Mahmud bin Mat (1954), p. 9, says 'there were no large agricultural developments or any other industry in those days'. Referring to the situation after debt-bondage had been abolished in Pahang the Dato' writes 'at the age of nine or ten the writer had, after school hours, to bear his share of the household drudgery while the elder members of the family had to bear the full burden of the labour on the farm which was formerly done by the slaves'.

The Dato', a Pahang aristocrat by birth, was formerly *Mentri Besar* (Chief Minister) of Pahang and then Speaker of the Federal Legislative Council.

this class of people in bondage had more cause for complaint than any other. For example one of them said:

> 'Our chief works are cooking, nursing, carrying water, splitting firewood, pounding rice, and at nights we are to prostitute ourselves giving half of this earning to the Raja and half to supply ourselves with clothing and provisions for the Sultan's house and other slaves. If we fail to get money by prostitution we are punished with thick rattans, and sometimes with canes on our heads and backs. We are prevented from marrying anyone who wishes to offer us in marriage.'[1]

There is some doubt as to the extent to which prostitution was voluntary or was forced upon them.[2] It was clearly of common occurrence except among the women reserved as concubines of the creditor.

This female retinue was kept as the means of satisfying the sexual appetites of the young, unmarried men who formed the chief's armed following. A chief thus gained two objects. He had the means of attracting to him men in search of mistresses and ultimately of wives. Secondly by providing his followers with the means of satisfying their sexual needs at home the chief prevented them from making forays among his peasant subjects to seduce or abduct their women. No doubt the chief had first to abduct some of these women himself under a more or less legal procedure. But this method was to be preferred to allowing his followers to make raids of their own. If they had done so, the chief's peasant subjects would either have fought back or more probably would have fled. In either case the chief would have been the poorer.

It was a recognized custom that a follower might ask his chief to give him a wife from among the women in his household.[3] There is also evidence that a Sultan, and possibly a district chief, had a right of control over the marriages of all women in the village in which he lived.[4]

A female follower who became a concubine of her master and bore him a child was said to be entitled to her freedom.[5] She must at least have achieved higher status in bondage in that way.

[1] *PCE.*

[2] J. W. W. Birch (*SSD*, 16 October 1875) reported that 'Prostitution is, I believe, forced upon them, but, in every case is encouraged by the creditor or master and in the generality of cases half the earnings are taken by the wives and concubines of the creditor.'

Low (slavery report dated 1 July, 1882) said that he knew of no case of enforced prostitution in Perak.

[3] See passage quoted above at p. 99.

[4] This is a deduction from a celebrated case at Bandar, the royal capital of Perak in 1875. The story is told in *PCE* (it is also briefly mentioned by Wilkinson and Winstedt (1934), p. 111). Birch, the British Resident, authorized the marriage of one of his servants, a Muslim Singhalese, to a woman of Bandar. It was considered an infringement of the Sultan's rights. No Malays of Bandar would attend the wedding and the necessary witnesses to the ceremony were Malay artisans then in Bandar but by origin from Penang. The corollary of the Sultan's right was that if the woman were divorced he might be required to provide for her support. It is uncertain how general this custom was.

[5] *PCE.*

Entry into debt-bondage was not always the unwelcome result of mis-fortune. It was observed that some 'voluntarily contracted debts when they knew well that it would lead to bondage'.[1]

If it is a fair conclusion that the average bondsman could look forward to reasonably good treatment and friendly relations with his creditor,[2] it is surprising only that men would thus surrender their liberty and run the risk of encountering a bad master. The most likely explanation is that many followers of chiefs were men without a home. It was a period of migration and instability. A part of the population was mere flotsam and jetsam in a hostile world. In these circumstances a homeless man might be tempted to attach himself in bondage to a chief. He thus got a living, the protection of a powerful patron, access to women and the ultimate prospect of obtaining a wife.[3] In this case, as in so many other relationships, the tie arose not so much from strength on one side and weakness on the other, as from mutual need. The follower needed a patron, a living and a wife. But the chief on his side needed a private army.

SLAVES

Much of what has been said of debt-bondsmen applies equally to slaves. British administrators tended to classify the two groups together as 'debt-slaves'.

There were however certain differences. A slave was lower in status than a debt-bondsman who ranked as a free man (*orang merdeka*). A Malay observer states:

'While there was no difference in the nature of the work which the two classes of slaves were made to do for their masters, the debt slaves were less degrading (*sic*) than the ordinary slaves because the former were supposed to be able to redeem themselves by paying off their debts whereas the latter could not under any circumstances regain their freedom except by some act of grace on the part of their master.'[4]

The right of self-redemption was however only rarely exercised.[5] The real distinction of status lay in the fact that debt-bondsmen (but not slaves) were still acknowledged as members of the same society as their masters. The distinction was rationalized by a rule which forbade the enslavement of Muslims by Muslims. Slaves therefore were mainly Africans, aborigines and Bataks (a non-Muslim Sumatran tribe).

[1] Swettenham (1948), p. 143.　　　　　　　[2] See above, pp. 100–1.

[3] There is to this day a preponderance of males and therefore a conscious shortage of women among immigrants from Indonesia. Thus the 1947 census gave the total of 43,560 'Other Malaysian' males in Selangor and 37,401 females. The figures of the first proper Selangor census held in 1891 are 1,925 males and 903 females.

[4] Dato' Mahmud bin Mat (1954), p. 9.

[5] See above, p. 99.

There was a hierarchy of status even in bondage. A non-Muslim foreigner could be enslaved. A Muslim Malay peasant could not be enslaved but he could be reduced to debt-bondage. At the next higher level an impecunious aristocrat who became indebted to his patron was not usually treated as a debt-bondsman. Of the only such case which has been traced it was said by a son of the creditor that 'a man like him is not expected to do menial work. He has opportunities of trading on his own account, and the only way his master requires his services is that he is obliged to attend on him.'[1] In effect an aristocrat could be a debtor but was not regarded as a debt-bondsman. It is an example of the pervasiveness of the status concept in the Malay social system.

THE NUMBER OF DEBTORS AND SLAVES

There are few exact data on the numbers of debtors and slaves. The best figures are the result of a census in Perak in 1879:[2]

Status	Male	Female
Free	24,188	23,171
Slaves	775	895
Debt-bondsmen	728	652

In Kedah in 1909 it was estimated that there were some 1,200 debt-bondsmen.[3]

In Selangor the number of bondsmen and slaves was certainly less than in Perak because there were fewer chiefs and the Malay population was much smaller.[4] In Negri Sembilan the size of the Malay population and the number of chiefs was approximately comparable with Perak. Except at the royal palace at Sri Menanti however there were few bondsmen or slaves in Negri Sembilan. This apparent discrepancy in Negri Sembilan is to be explained in terms of the different social conditions of that State. The population was more homogeneous and longer settled. There were fewer homeless fighting men in search of a patron. The district chiefs and clan heads had ties of kinship (or pseudo-kinship) with their peasant subjects and could mobilize a levy as required. Along the Linggi River however conditions more nearly approached those of other States and here each major notable had a stockade and a following of professional fighting men—but recruited by marrying them to local women rather than as debt-bondsmen.

---

[1] *PCE.*

[2] *SSD,* 4 May 1882. At this time the British regime still tolerated slavery and debt-bondage as legal institutions. But three years of the *pax Britannica* had removed most of the inducement to maintain private armies. The two largest creditors of bondsmen were women—a sign that it was no longer a military institution. The Regent of Perak and two or three other chiefs refused to allow their households to be counted.

[3] *AR Kedah,* 1909.   [4] See above, p. 23 and 91.

H

THE CHIEF AT WORK

The account so far given of the district chief shows him as the focus of
what may be called a 'power group'. He has a circle of aristocratic aides
and hangers-on who assist him in the work which he and they may do
without loss of status. He has a small standing force of fighting men at
his back. He has a number of agricultural workers and women at his
disposal whose services meet the sexual, domestic and alimentary needs
of the group. The group is bound to him by ties of compulsion and of
reciprocal self-interest.

The chief and his group are only a small proportion of the population.
Nonetheless they are the source of its leadership in many fields. To trace
the operation of that leadership in every sphere would require a lengthy
study of many aspects of Malay society at that time. Such a full-length
study is not attempted here. The remainder of this section of the book
and the two sections which follow deal more particularly with the political
aspects of leadership in administration, law and defence with a brief
account of the large subject of Malay economic organization.

A chief, or one of his close kinsmen, acted as village headman of the
village in which the chief resided. He exercised authority over outlying
villages through the headmen of each village. The working of the system
is best illustrated by the preparations of the Maharaja Lela of Pasir Salak
(in Perak) for an attack on the British Resident of Perak, J. W. W. Birch,
in 1875.[1] The district of Pasir Salak was about midway between the upper
and lower reaches of the Perak River. The Maharaja Lela was one of the
'Eight Chiefs' (i.e. a chief of the second rank) but he was one of the
strongest personalities in Perak at this time. He had various personal
reasons for hating Birch but the mainspring of his activity was his convic-
tion that the newly established British Protectorate would deprive him
and his fellow chiefs of their power.

When he had decided to revolt the Maharaja Lela's first move was to
strengthen the stockade and ditch which formed his strong-point at Pasir
Salak. He convened a meeting of his subjects and announced that a stockade and ditch were to be built (previously he had had a fence round his
house which was of no defensive value). Each villager was required to
provide 100 pieces of wood for the stockade and to erect five fathoms of
it. Alternatively he could pay $5 in lieu of working and $1 instead of
providing wood. Some villagers paid and others worked. Defaulters were
fined $25. The money which the Maharaja Lela received was used to

[1] Birch was killed at Pasir Salak on 2 November 1875. The revolt for which
this attack was to be the signal failed to materialize. The Maharaja Lela was
eventually caught and hung. There was a full-scale enquiry into the causes of the
attack and the unsuccessful plan for a revolt. The records of that enquiry and of
the trial of the Maharaja Lela are the source of much information used in this
book.

employ paid Javanese labourers on work requiring special skill or unusual exertion. The work lasted two or three months. A witness said:

> 'There were constant feasts given by the Maharaja Lela while the work was going on, every second or third day a buffalo was killed. As soon as the stockade was finished a big feast was given at which there were more than three hundred people present and a daughter of the Maharaja Lela had her ears pierced.'[1]

The Sultan of Perak and the major chiefs were invited to the final feast. The piercing of a girl's ears is a ceremony to mark the onset of puberty.

The finished work was a ditch twelve feet broad and six feet deep filled with water from the river; an earth embankment; and a high wooden fence surmounting the embankment. In such cases the fence was usually a double line of timber stakes with earth rammed down in the space between. Such a fence was impervious to musket balls and possibly to rifle fire.

The next move was to convene a meeting at the Maharaja Lela's house at which the headmen and notables of the district, and also a chief of lower status from across the river, were present, together with a large concourse of the common people. One of them said:

> 'According to Perak custom on the occasion of an assembly only the people of rank would be allowed to enter a Dato's house. On ordinary occasions of course I might enter.'[2]

The Maharaja Lela produced to the meeting a letter from the Sultan and gave it to his father-in-law, Pandak Indut, to read out. These proceedings took place in semi-publicity on the open verandah of the house; the commoners sat or stood outside; a dozen of the Javanese labourers were sitting eating their rice indifferent to a matter of no concern to them. The Sultan's letter authorized an attack on the British Residency at Bandar Bahru.

> 'When the letter had been read, Maharaja Lela took a coat, a pair of trousers and a head handkerchief. He gave them to Pandak Indut who put them on. He took a sword and put it under Pandak Indut's arm. The Maharaja Lela said, "I have got a name (sc. a chiefly title), Pandak Indut has none, but this shall be a sign that you shall follow him. Whatever Pandak Indut says, do." Then all the people went away.'[2]

It so happened that Birch was coming to Pasir Salak. It was therefore decided to kill him there rather than attack him at the Residency at Bandar Bahru. Pandak Indut and two other notables made a plan for attacking Birch when his launch was tied up at the river bank. For this purpose they divided their followers into three parties. The Maharaja Lela's brother, Ngah Ja'afar, distributed arms among the men chosen for the attack. The Maharaja Lela himself took no part in the attack. But this

---

[1] *PCE.*

[2] Proceedings of the Maharaja Lela's trial sent to London under cover of *SSD*, 11 January 1877.

may have been a deviation from the normal conduct of a chief intended to enable him to disclaim responsibility if things went wrong.

There are some points of general significance in this narrative. The mobilization of labour for the construction of the ditch and the stockade was an example of the customary corvée system known as *kerah* which Swettenham describes as follows:

> 'When a chief wanted labour for any public or private work—such as the clearing of a river, the building of a mosque or house, the manning of boats for a journey—all the men within reach were summoned, through the village headmen, to come and undertake this forced labour, for which no payment was ever made, and though the labourers were supposed to be fed as long as the work lasted, that was not always done.'[1]

There was no restriction on the type of work which a chief might thus commission. The distinction between 'public works' and labour for the private benefit of the chief was not in the Malay habit of thinking of this time.

There was no restriction on the duration of these services or on the season of the year at which they might be required. A man might, for example, be required to attend on his chief during an absence of several months on a visit to the State capital.

In practice however there were definite limitations. If men were called away at the harvest season it was a hardship which was particularly resented.[2] In such a case, or if food was not regularly provided, the labour force would melt away before the work was completed. It will be noted that the Maharaja Lela went to some expense to provide a regular supply of buffalo meat (something of a luxury). There is an interesting comparative case in Perak in January 1875. The Sultan asked a conclave of chiefs to build a hall for his ceremonial installation. Each chief sent out a working party to cut timber. Only those chiefs who provided the full ration scale (rice, fish and betel nut) were able to produce their quota of timber.[3]

In effect a chief could not mobilize labour for a large task unless he had the resources with which to feed it. This was an important limitation and a factor of significance in connexion with the accumulation of readily available resources by chiefs.

The *kerah* system was an occasion for making distinctions of status. No aristocrat was required to turn out to do such work. Among the commoner class certain categories of higher status than the rest were exempt. The most detailed code of these exemption rules comes from Kedah.[4] Those exempted were any *Raja* (aristocrat), *Syed* (descendant of the Prophet), any other person 'of good birth', a *Haji* (returned pilgrim to Mecca), *lebai* (Muslim divine), *pegawai* (government official), *penghulu*

---

[1] Swettenham (1948), p. 143.   [2] *SSD*, 15 October 1887.

[3] *PCE*.

[4] *AR Kedah*, 1909. The obligation to work had been commuted to a land tax but exemptions were granted on the old basis.

(village headman), mosque official, servant of the Sultan's household or any other person individually exempted. Kedah in 1909 was much more of a settled bureaucracy than Perak in 1870 and it may be doubted if the Perak exemption system was neatly detailed to this extent. But the principle of exemption as a mark of status was the same.

The significance of constructing a secure base, in the form of a stockade and a ditch, will be discussed in connexion with Malay warfare.[1]

The appointment of Pandak Indut as commander for the attack was made with maximum publicity at a meeting convened for that purpose. The delegation of authority was marked by the formal transfer of a suit of clothes and a weapon. The power and authority of a chief were a personal attribute and had thus to be symbolically transferred. The sword and the suit of clothes were customary symbols of the authority of the chief. When the chief was first appointed the Sultan gave him a sword; at his death the sword was formally and publicly returned to the Sultan in token that the office conferred upon him for life had expired.[2] It is still the custom in Negri Sembilan that a newly appointed district chief (*Undang*) brings a suit of clothes to the Yam Tuan among other customary gifts.[3]

The public reading of the Sultan's letter is an example of the practice of treating the receipt of an official letter as a major political event.[4]

The whole ceremony took place in the fore-part of the Maharaja Lela's house. All Malay houses, whatever the status of the owner, were and still are built to comprise three main elements. At the front is the place where visitors are received and any public act (e.g. a village wedding) takes place. The central portion is the living and sleeping space. It is reserved particularly to the women. Women visitors, but not usually men, may be admitted to this part of the house if they are relatives or close friends. At night male visitors sleep in the front part of the house and women visitors in the central part. The rear portion of the house is the kitchen.

In the house of a villager the fore-portion is no more than a verandah (*serambi*). A village headman or man of wealth may have a projecting fore-room (*anjong*). In the case of a chief or Sultan this section of the house is a hall of audience (*balai*). If the hall of audience is particularly large it may be subdivided into sections by lines of pillars.[5] The portion nearest

---

[1] See below, p. 121.

[2] *SSD*, 11 January 1877. *AR Pk*, 1906, for an example of the return of a sword.

[3] I have been told that the clothes are supposed to have belonged to the late chief and are sent as a symbol of his decease.

[4] See above, p. 52.

[5] The lines of pillars were made necessary by the limitations of Malay technology which could not build roof spans of more than a certain size. The interesting fact is the use of the pillars as divisions between units of Malay 'socio-spacial categories' (Evans-Pritchard (1940), p. 109).

the front is open to commoners; the middle and rear portions of the hall are reserved for important people and for the family of the house.

These arrangements are almost self-explanatory. All classes lived their public lives in the fore-part of the house. The public lives of the ruling class consisted of acts of state.

Istana of Sultan Yusuf of Perak at Sayong (c.1885)

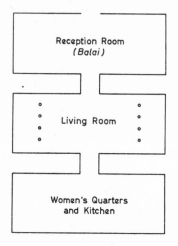

This drawing is based only on a brief description by Swettenham.[1] The building is said to have consisted of three palm-thatched buildings joined by gangways. In front was the ante-room for the reception of visitors. The centre building had wooden pillars dividing off verandahs on either side. The third building in the rear was the women's quarters and kitchen.

The diagram on page 111 is copied (dimensions approximate) from a plan included in the papers of the Commission of Enquiry into the Perak War of 1875–6. This was probably the house of the headman of Batak Rabit in which the Sultan resided for a short period at the end of 1874. Owing to an outbreak of cholera he lived in boats at various places on the Perak River during most of 1875. The lay-out is atypical but the usual elements are to be seen: (1) reception room, bottom right; (2) Sultan's quarters, top right.

When a large assembly was held, the part of the house reserved for public affairs served as a platform for the notables. The common people were denied access and remained outside at ground level.[2] The correlation

---

[1] Swettenham (1895), pp. 147 and 151.

[2] All Malay houses are built on 'stilts' and the floor-level (there is only one storey except for a sort of loft) is four to six feet above ground-level. This is a necessary precaution in houses built on the banks of rivers which flood on occasion.

Istana of Sultan Abdullah of Perak at Batak Rabit (1874)

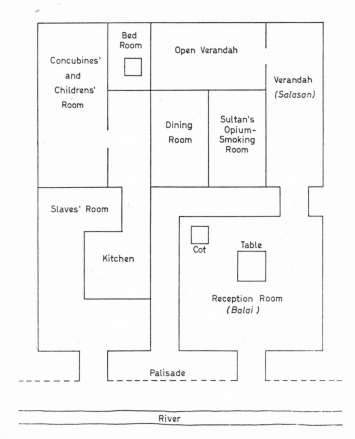

of height (of sitting position) with dignity is common enough in Malay culture. At installation ceremonies a Sultan or chief is seated cross-legged upon a dais of a prescribed number of tiers according to the dignity of his office.

There is another aspect of the social significance of Malay chiefs' houses which deserves mention. Houses were a mark of status. The Maharaja Lela was particularly proud of his house which was 'the best in Perak'.[1] The wealthy chiefs of Larut (Perak) and Lukut (Selangor) had houses built of brick (in contrast to the usual style in timber). The significance of a Sultan's residence has already been mentioned.[2] The

[1] *PCE*. Sultan Ismail of Perak had given him money towards the cost of building it and he held himself particularly obligated to the Sultan for that reason.

[2] See above, p. 63—especially the quotation about the Sultan's house and his dignity.

outward form as well as the size and style of the house denoted status. For example in Perak only the three holders of royal offices (Sultan, Raja Muda and Raja Bendahara) might have a house with a two-tier roof.[1] Lesser Rajas and chiefs (but not persons of lower degree) might have houses with concave roof-trees.

[1] Winstedt (1909). There is a rich Malay vocabulary of terms for architectural features of houses. See, e.g. Wilkinson (1932), item *balai*. These terms relate to the structure of aristocrats' houses and reflect the preoccupation with status implicit in this subject.

6

Law and War

It is an essential function of a political system that it should afford to the community in which it exists a necessary minimum of internal order and of protection against external attack. It is not necessary or possible that there should be complete tranquillity. In many societies the political order is built upon the existence of groups which are themselves held together as groups partly by their opposition to each other. In an extreme case, such as the Nuer, this factor may be the main element in the political system. In other societies, including the Malay States, inter-group opposition was only one factor among several. Its presence in any degree however serves to illustrate the proposition that political order may be based in part on forces of disorder. The situation to be expected is then a balance between order and disorder rather than a perfect state of order.

It was in this sphere of law and order that the Malay subject class was able to check an abuse or failure of the exercise of power by its rulers. Justice and order to a superlative degree was not expected. But if it dropped below a certain minimum level the bases of power were sapped away.

A chief had to hold and if possible to increase the population of his district. Population was the source of his wealth (as a tax-collector) and therefore of his ability to maintain an armed following as the basis of his power. It was by no means inevitable that the population of his district would remain or increase. If he oppressed them unduly or failed to protect them against marauders, the people would flee away and settle elsewhere. The essential mobility of Malay peasant settlement has been explained.[1] It was a reflection of the political and the economic circumstances of the time. In some societies land is scarce or has a special value so that a ruler who can allot land may be sure of attracting and holding subjects by that means. Where land is not a scarce commodity however, and this was the case in the Malay States,[2] political power even though it is exercised in respect of defined territorial areas is based on control of people. The sanction against injustice in court and defeat in battle was loss of manpower.

[1] See above, pp. 28–9.

[2] 'Land had no value in the Malay States of 1874 and it was the custom for anyone to settle where he pleased on unoccupied and unclaimed land.' Swettenham (1948), p. 136.

LAW AND ORDER

As a preliminary to discussing Malay law as a means of social control it
is necessary to distinguish and dismiss Malay law as literature. There are
extant several Malay legal codes compiled at various times from the fifteenth to the nineteenth centuries. These codes have been printed,
translated and commented upon at some length.[1] They are of interest as
showing the extent to which Arabic legal theory was absorbed into Malay
culture as a result of the conversion of the Malays to Islam. The codes
were however only the work of learned scribes at the courts of Sultans.
No one ever referred to the codes, of which copies were very rare, for
guidance in settling a dispute. The leading European authority on Malay
law has warned against taking 'the so-called codes too seriously'.[2] The
first British administrator sent to Pahang (and also a leading authority
on Malay culture) wrote:

> 'No penal code of any kind is in existence except the old Malay *kanun* which
> allows no fine under two ounces of gold, and is more curious as an antiquity
> than useful as a practical guide to governing the country. So rough indeed is
> this code that many of the most ordinary offences are not mentioned therein,
> and many of the punishments, such as cutting off the right hand for pilfering,
> are too barbarous for use even in Pahang. Added to this that hardly anyone
> except a few Malay scholars know the contents of the *kanun*, and that it is never
> followed in dealing with offences, and it may fairly be said that no code of laws
> exists in Pahang.'[3]

It did happen occasionally that an aristocrat learned in the codes sat in
judgment and tried to apply them.[4] The more general situation is described
thus:

> 'Theoretically all local administration was governed by these laws, but if
> any one of the latter happened to clash with the ideas or with the inclinations of
> any individual who was strong enough to set it at defiance, there existed no
> power that was able to compel obedience.'[5]

It may be concluded that there was no written law in the Malay States
of any significance as established law.

The rules applied in the maintenance of internal order and the granting
of remedies for wrongs can best be understood as an aspect of the political
system in operation. The concept of a judiciary independent of the executive and acting occasionally as a check upon it was absent from the Malay

[1] The best-known is *The Ninety-Nine Laws of Perak* edited and translated by
J. Rigby (1908). Wilkinson (1908b) is the best and most realistic commentator.
See also Winstedt (1947a), pp. 87–102.

[2] Wilkinson (1908b), p. 3.

[3] *SSD*, 1 October 1887 (Hugh Clifford).

[4] *PSC*, 6 September 1878, records that the law of Perak was unwritten though
it appeared to differ little from the written codes. Raja Dris, a man of learning,
had been appointed chief judge in 1876 under the British regime. He was a member
of the State Council and the opinion cited above was probably his.

[5] Sir Hugh Clifford in his opening speech to the F.M.S. Federal Council in 1927.

States at this time. Sultans and chiefs administered the law as part of their function of preserving order. In a sense all law was *droit administratif*.

There was a close correspondence between (1) the content of the law and the machinery for its enforcement and (2) the distribution of political power. The important political institutions were the village headman, the district chief and, as a weak paramount above the district chiefs, the Sultan of the State. There was a corresponding hierarchy of judicial authority. The village headman was responsible for the maintenance of law and order in his village and for the arrest of offenders. The extent to which he was a judge (as distinct from a conciliator) is discussed below. He had at least to keep the peace. The more serious offenders were handed over to the district chief. A district chief had theoretical power to deal only with offences which were not capital.[1] It appears however that a chief was acting within his jurisdiction if he dealt with a capital offence but did not impose a capital penalty. It was the power to order judicial execution which was supposed to be reserved to the Sultan. On the same principle a chief was supposed to remit to the Sultan any fine in excess of $25, the nominal 'blood money' value of a human life.

In practice the chiefs usurped the powers of the Sultan. They tried any cases which they pleased, passed such sentences as they wished, and kept all fines.[2] In effect there were only two levels or types of court. There was village justice administered or directed by the village headman as leader of a community to which he himself belonged. Secondly there was the justice of the ruling class exercised over their subjects.

There was a corresponding division in the content of the law. Village law (if 'law' be the appropriate term) was Indonesian custom. No doubt the details of this custom varied between villages settled by immigrants from different parts of Indonesia.[3] The best-known of these local customary codes was the Negri Sembilan custom known as the '*adat perpateh*, derived from the Menangkabau custom of Sumatra. The same custom was apparently the basis of much village practice in Perak where the Menangkabau influence although not dominant was stronger than any other.

In parallel with the village custom and to some extent superimposed above it was the law of Sultans and chiefs. This law was the exercise of authority of rulers over subjects. Its historical derivation was through the Malacca Sultanate to the authoritarianism of the Hindu kingdoms.

[1] Wilkinson (1908b) lists the following as capital offences: treason, incest, robbery, arson, theft, cheating, poisoning, stabbing and murder.

[2] For example in Pahang 'Many of the local chiefs, especially those residing in the more remote districts . . . formerly exercised in the absence of the Sultan a practically unlimited jurisdiction in civil and criminal cases, although they were supposed to send all cases of murder to Pekan.' *AR Phg*, 1888.

[3] 'Customary law differed widely in various parts of the Peninsula.' Sir Hugh Clifford in his speech to the F.M.S. Federal Council in 1927.

In Negri Sembilan the chieftainship was an office filled by election from below; the powers of chiefs were therefore circumscribed. The royal ruler of Negri Sembilan had few powers indeed. In this State therefore the *'adat perpateh*, the local village custom, flourished and even invaded the sphere of relations between rulers and subjects. Elsewhere aristocratic authority reshaped village custom *in so far as* the chiefs were concerned with it all. Thus Wilkinson could say that the differences between the Negri Sembilan custom (*'adat perpateh*) and the custom or law (*'adat temenggong*) of the other States were 'superficial and are connected with the way the law is administered rather than with the actual law itself'.[1] He also remarked that the custom of States other than Negri Sembilan was 'the *'adat perpateh* administered on aristocratic lines'.[2] A code of law must mean different things according to the status of the judges.

It is doubtful whether village law should be called 'law' at all by the test of law as rules enforced by 'organized legal sanctions'.[3] The Malay village headman was indeed concerned to enforce the custom but the sanctions employed were hardly legal. The headman had but a single constable (the *Mata-Mata*) through whom to exert his authority. If he gave a decision which was unwelcome to a majority of the village, his authority might well be defied. If he inflicted injustice on a minority, he ran the risk of losing that section of his village community—they would go elsewhere. He had thus to conciliate and to carry the leading men of the village with him. Equally the individual villager had to submit to what his fellows recognized as a fair judgment—or quit the village. The sanction was the sheer impossibility of living together in a village unless occasional disputes could be settled by the agreed application of a traditional penalty or compensation.

Lack of evidence (in itself a significant fact) makes it impossible to establish this view of Malay village legal processes as a matter of proven fact. But British administrators noted that:

'In the country districts, which are inhabited by purely agricultural classes, there is little or no crime.'[4]

No crime came the way of their court system. They inferred that there was none. It seems more likely that what little crime did occur could be settled within the village. On the other hand it was found that crime among Malays did come to notice in large towns and in and around the mining districts. In such cases the sanctions of village life did not apply and the temptations to wrong-doing were perhaps stronger.

There are scattered references to the sort of wrongs which gave rise to village disputes. These include damage to crops by straying buffaloes,

---

[1] Wilkinson (1908b). [2] Wilkinson, op. cit.

[3] Radcliffe-Brown (1952), p. 212. [4] *AR Phg*, 1897.

personal injury either deliberate or accidental, slander, cattle theft, adultery and the like.[1]

Law as administered by chiefs served to preserve control over subjects and to maintain the 'King's Peace' in which all rulers had an interest. The chiefs also used their legal powers to transfer wealth from their subjects to themselves by the imposition of fines which were an important source of revenue. A heavy fine was also a means of reducing a free man to the status of a debt-bondsman.

Among particular cases there is mention of a headman in Rembau (Negri Sembilan) fined because his people did not attend when the chief called them.[2] The Sultan of Pahang fined a subject for forgetting to bring the Sultan's dagger; another for marrying without his consent; and a third for allowing a dove to escape which he was about to present to the Sultan[3]. A chief in Perak fined a man $100 for lifting the ends of his trousers clear of the mud as he passed in front of the chief's house.[4] These are instances of *lèse majesté* rather than of judicial decisions.

For court work there were no special staff, no special place of trial and no rules of procedure. There were no expert assessors or advisers learned in the law. A chief of lesser status sat in judgment himself and gave audience in his house as the need arose. A Sultan or a great chief might delegate the hearing of cases to a kinsman together with the right to keep all or a part of the court fines. Rules of evidence were confined to a few proverbial maxims. There was no recognized obligation to give a hearing to both parties.

> 'When cases arise, if the people in question live near Pekan, one of them goes and complains to the Bendahara or one of his familiars, and sentence is passed without any enquiry being made of the party against whom the complaint is made.'[5]

These instances quoted on this and the previous page come from the reports of British administrators. No doubt they recorded the facts accurately as far as their knowledge went. But the picture is incomplete. No society could have held together if such arbitrary oppression was all that served to regulate relations between rulers and subjects.

Part of the compensatory balance of the system has been mentioned.[6]

---

[1] One such case is related thus: 'She was passing by a village and met an acquaintance, with whom she stopped to converse. Taking a stone from the roadside she placed it on the pathway, and sat down to rest meanwhile. When she left the spot she passed on her way and thought no more of the stone. About an hour afterwards a child from the village came running along the path, and accidentally tripped over the stone, fell and slightly cut its forehead.' This led to a fine of $25. *SSD*, 6 April 1875.

[2] *SSD*, 28 February 1883.   [3] *SSD*, 28 June 1884.

[4] Swettenham (1951), p. 118. To lift the sarong is an indecent gesture and most offensive. In the case mentioned above it was of course a gross abuse of power based on a mere technicality.

[5] *SSD*, 1 October 1887.   [6] See above, p. 113.

A chief who oppressed all his people or even the most influential of them could lose them from his district. There can be no doubt that arbitrary acts of oppression did occur. What is less certain is the extent to which the instances cited in the administrative reports were typical. It was the people with a grievance who went to complain to the British officials in the early days of the protectorate regime. It seems likely that the instances reported were not entirely representative.

Moreover the chief had always to take into account that the individual whom he oppressed had a recognized way of hitting back. He could 'run amuck'[1] killing all who crossed his path before he himself was cornered and cut down. Such retaliation might not reach the chief person-ally—it was the essence of running amuck (*mengamok*) that the killer was half insane and would even kill his own family and friends without recognition or any consciousness of retaliating against his oppressor. But a chief would not wish to provoke such a violent breach of his own law and order.

A chief had every inducement not to antagonize his armed following and the peasantry upon whom he depended for his wealth and power. He might oppress particular individuals with impunity but not the mass of his subjects. To the generality of the subject class of his district he had to dispense rough justice in accordance with the custom. In addition he had to protect his subjects or get them retribution if any other chief or potentate did them wrong. This aspect of the system was expressed as follows:

> 'At its best it encouraged a chief to assist his own followers against the stranger. It never put a premium on the chief doing justice to the stranger at the cost of his own men. In a country district where the people all acknowledged one common territorial chief, justice might be honestly administered. But in places where rival magnates existed the quarrels of their followers were simply passed on to their patrons.'[2]

The concept of justice in such circumstances must be reconsidered. The European mechanism of justice is the application of a fixed code of law in accordance with precedent and without fear or favour to all whom an independent judiciary have to adjudicate between. In the light of experience it may be reasonable to claim that this mechanism is the most efficient means to the end of giving impartial justice to all.[3] But this mechanism is the product of an unusual sequence of conditions

[1] See above, p. 74, n. 3.   [2] Wilkinson (1908b), p. 43.

[3] There is a remarkable tribute to European law in the course of 500 pages of sometimes bitter criticism of European influence in Asia in K. M. Panikkar (1953), p. 497: 'The establishment of the great principle of equality of all before law in a country where under Hindu doctrines a Brahmin could not be punished on the evidence of a Sudra, or even punishments varied according to caste, and where, according to Muslim law, testimony could not be accepted against a Muslim was itself a legal revolution of the first importance . . . the Indian penal code was a great improvement on the previous systems.'

and events. Its usefulness has been denied even in Europe by the fascist and communist regimes of the past generation. In many parts of the world it has never existed at all—or only as a European importation.

The more common mechanism for the settlement of wrongs and disputes is the exercise of power by political authorities in accordance with the distribution of power between them and subject only to the indirect sanction that a political system which disintegrates its own society works its own destruction. The essential function of law and order is to preserve social cohesion. An attempt to elevate justice into an absolute thing and not something relative to the society in which it exists leads on to Platonic abstractions—not that it is necessarily wrong on that account.

Thus in a Malay State a peasant had a moderate expectation of justice at the hands of his own chief because the chief could not afford to disintegrate the population of his district by a *general* course of oppression or injustice beyond what the conventions of the relationship between ruler and subject permitted. In his relations with people outside the district, whether aristocrats or commoners, the peasant looked to the chief to get justice for him.

The next question is—what was the mechanism for regulating relations between chief and chief in the cases when they quarrelled over personal issues or the affairs of individual subjects? In theory it was the function of the Sultan as the fount of all justice and the embodiment of the unity of the State to keep the chiefs in order and to do justice between them. In practice the Sultans were rarely strong enough to compel a turbulent chief who was in the wrong to make amends. Swettenham tells a story of a chief who had assaulted a rival in a quarrel over a mistress:

'For this assault the ruler of the country . . . summoned his vassal into his presence to hear his sentence. The delinquent duly attended, and with an attitude and bearing required by the circumstances, listened to the statement of his misdeeds, in the presence of a very large number of fellow chiefs and less important people.'

The sentence was a fine of $2,000. The story ends:

'The chief bowed his acknowledgements in silence, and as he withdrew . . . it is said he whispered, "I was afraid His Highness would fine me fifty cents".'[1]

This episode occurred a few years after the British regime had been established in Perak. In more troubled times it may be doubted whether the wrong-doer would have submitted in this way.

The story serves however to illustrate a significant point. The chief submitted to formal humiliation before his Sultan and a heavy penalty rather than defy the Sultan. Any such defiance would be a challenge to the unity of the State rather than to the Sultan personally. Moreover it would deprive the rebel of his own charter of status since his office was a gift of the Sultan. It was customary to seek the approval of the Sultan even when the Sultan had no power to make his approval effective. The

[1] Swettenham (1900), p. 140.

most famous case was Sultan Adbul Samad, the *roi fainéant* of the Selangor civil war (1866–73) in which:

> 'Each party in turn and each individual leader made periodical visits to the old Sultan, complained bitterly of the other side, and asked for tin or money, arms and ammunition. To all comers, from whatever quarter, the Sultan seemed to signify his approval and, with strict impartiality, made gifts of some sort.'[1]

Another instance from Perak begins with the murder of chief A by a kinsman of chief B because chief A had denied justice to the murderer against one of his subjects. After the murder chief B, accepting responsibility for his kinsman, went to make his peace with the Sultan:

> 'Accompanied by all his people he went and stood in front of the Sultan's house with his hands loosely tied behind his back with his own head-kerchief and, thus uncovered in the sun, he and all his following shouted, "*Ampun, Tuanku, beribu-ribu ampun*", (Pardon, my lord, a thousand-thousand pardons). After a quarter of an hour's waiting, while the air was filled with this plea for mercy, and the Bendahara and his company stood like prisoners in front of the closed house, a door opened, a herald bearing the Sultan's insignia appeared and cried out, "Our Lord pardons you and permits you to enter his presence.'[2]

This procedure was called *ikat diri* (to bind oneself). The Sultan, having given formal pardon to one powerful faction, tried to pacify the other by conferring the chieftainship of the murdered man on his brother.

WARFARE

The lack of adequate machinery for keeping order between the chiefs explains the nature of Malay warfare at this time. Wars were fought as a means of 'self-help' to obtain revenge and also to adjust the balance of power within the State. Warfare between States did not occur at all— partly because the British 'sphere of influence' was sufficiently effective to prevent fighting without any active intervention (before 1874). When British policy changed to active intervention in the Malay States, there was, for the first time for two generations, a form of external (i.e. British) pressure evoking a Malay response in terms of national defence of the State. By that time however the organization of national defence had so withered away by disuse and by the effects of civil war that it would no longer function satisfactorily.

The typical situation was civil war between chiefs. In its simplest form one chief raided the territory of another for loot or to oust his opponent from his district. The more complex situations, such as the Selangor civil war of 1866–73, involved opposing coalitions of warring chiefs. The Selangor civil war may fairly be called a struggle between the 'Haves' and the 'Have Nots' for control of the important districts of the State. In Perak at about the same time there was a long-drawn struggle, which rarely broke out into open fighting, between two territorial coalitions,

[1] Swettenham (1948), p. 130.

[2] Swettenham (1895), pp. 112–46, 'The Passing of Panglima Perang Samaun'.

the Up-River (*Ulu*) and the Down-River (*Hilir*) chiefs, for control of the Sultanate. Each party supported its own candidate for the throne. In Negri Sembilan it was a struggle between the royal ruler (Yam Tuan) backed by some minor chiefs against the wealthiest of the major chiefs (the Dato' Klana of Sungei Ujong). In all cases the fruits of victory, and the real bone of contention, were the revenues to be obtained from export taxes on the output of Chinese mining areas. It thus happened that the struggles between Malay chiefs overlapped with strife between the Chinese miners for exclusive control of the richer tin deposits.

Even in civil wars between coalitions of chiefs the fighting was mostly a desultory affair of raids. The only long-drawn operations were the sieges of stockades. It is perhaps significant that there is a Malay proverb about the folly of sitting down to starve out the defenders of a fort without having sufficient provisions to outlast them.[1] Sieges were not common because of the essential commissariat difficulty of keeping a force in the field. The typical operation began with the departure of a raiding party which endeavoured to approach the enemy stockade unobserved so as to capture it by a single desperate rush before the defenders could rally. If these tactics failed or could not be employed, the attackers either withdrew or tried to take the stockade without severe fighting. They might, for example, resort to the stratagem of a mock attack which failed in the hope that the defenders, elated by the apparent victory, would sally forth in pursuit—and fall into an ambush. Determined attacks on prepared positions, with the inevitable consequence of heavy casualties, were not favoured. Victory at the price of a long list of killed and wounded would soon demoralize the followers of any leader who resorted to such tactics.

The stockades were the focal points of these struggles and manoeuvres. They were sited on the banks of rivers and often at the point of junction of a tributary and the main stream. They dominated the 'crossroads' of the river communications system. No attacking party could safely go past a stockade and leave it to cut off their line of retreat—if indeed they could get their boats, the essential means of transport, past the fort without being bombarded by the defenders. The stockade, once taken, gave control of a large area upstream or up the side valley. Any chief who expected to be involved in fighting, even if the first move was to be an attack launched by him elsewhere, put his defences in order first. This is the significance of the Maharaja Lela's activity in rebuilding his stockade at Pasir Salak before attacking the British Resident.[2]

The stockades consisted of an outer rampart of earth surmounted by a fence and encircled on the outside by a moat. Beyond the moat sharpened bamboo stakes were stuck in the ground with their points up at an angle to form caltrops (Malay *ranjau*) to cut the feet and legs of the attackers.

---

[1] *Pelabur habis, Palembang ta' alah.* Brown (1951), p. 142.

[2] See above, p. 106.

I

Stakes might also be put at the bottom of concealed pits to await the fall of the unwary. Further forward still trees were felled to form an abattis. Inside the rampart were the dwelling houses of the defenders; the walls of these buildings were strengthened to resist musket balls and were loopholed for firing. At the corners of the stockade, which was generally rectangular in shape, were projecting bastions (*kubu*) in which swivel cannon (*lela*) were mounted to take the attackers in enfilade as they approached the rampart. The gateway to the area within the stockade could be closed with a heavy gate. It was usual to have a small standing guard in a gatehouse to forestall a surprise rush. In one stockade at least[1] there was a trench leading out from the rear of the stockade so that the defenders could get away unobserved if discretion seemed the better part of valour. This same stockade was found to contain a considerable stock of rice as stores for a siege.

The tactics already described were very reasonable in view of the advantages enjoyed by the defenders. The attackers had no artillery with which to breach the stockade before making their attack. Cannon were used only in defence probably because they were too heavy to be carried by raiding parties travelling light.[2] For the most part the fighting man used only the weapons which he could carry. These were the dagger (*keris*), sword (*pedang*), throwing spear (*lembing*) and the rifle or musket (*senapang*). In the 1870's the musket, matchlock or flintlock, was still the most common type of firearm. Snider rifles were however coming into use.

Daggers and knives were still made in the Malay States but many were also imported from Sumatra. Gunpowder and bullets (of tin) could at a pinch be made locally. But the greater part of the weapons and munitions of war had to be purchased abroad and imported.

At this point it is convenient to pass on to consider some political aspects of Malay warfare. The provision of weapons, more especially firearms, and of ammunition, supplies and money for the maintenance of a fighting force was the responsibility of the chief who initiated the military action to be taken. In the case of the Maharaja Lela[3] it will be noted that he provided the weapons for the attack on Birch. Previously the Maharaja Lela had obtained muskets, gunpowder, rice and money from the Sultan both as a token of approval and as material support for his action.

Initiative in warfare was thus closely linked with control of economic resources. There were comparatively few chiefs with the means to sustain military operations on a relatively large scale. The few who had such resources were the inevitable foci of coalitions financed by themselves. Fighting was a form of political action since it was part of an internal struggle for power within the State. The military initiative could be

---

[1] The stockade of the Dato' Bandar of Sungei Ujong at Kepayang (near the modern Seremban) captured by British forces in 1874. *SSD*, 29 December 1874.

[2] For the use of Malay cannon in attack by a European, see Gullick (1954).

[3] See above, p. 107.

taken by chiefs of exceptional wealth and power even though they were not themselves redoubtable warriors. Conversely military prowess was not automatically a source of political power since prowess alone was valueless without the sinews of war.

The association of arms with political power made weapons an index of prestige. Cannon were accumulated not as artillery but for display or as a convenient means of capital accumulation.[1] An observer noted of the Malays 'the extraordinary passion they exhibit for carrying arms'.[2] Swettenham commented:

> 'In 1874 every Malay had as many weapons as he could carry; say two daggers in his belt, two spears in his hand, a gun over his shoulder, and a long sword under his arm.'[3]

On appointment a chief was given a weapon, usually a sword, as the symbol of his office.[4] When the Maharaja Lela publicly delegated authority to Pandak Indut he invested him with his sword.[5] A Sultan or a great chief sent out a herald with his sword as the symbol of his authority, e.g. for collecting a tax or rounding up women.[6] A Malay chief could marry a secondary wife by sending his dagger (keris) in token of his presence at the ceremony.[7]

There were elaborate beliefs in the magical efficacy of weapons. At its more prosaic level this attitude appeared in the special value placed on a weapon known to have taken human life. For example Sultan Abdullah of Perak gave the Maharaja Lela a keris worth $400 'on account of many people having been killed by it'.[8] The 'luck' of a weapon depended on its possessing certain proportions and markings.[9]

This situation would seem to be a form of symbolism. Weapons were naturally associated with fighting and fighting with the exercise of power. Thus weapons became one of the symbols of political office. The magical beliefs perhaps derived from the uncertainties of war—the fighting man ever seeks the assurance of invulnerability and of victory. But it is notable that the magical lore of weapons tended to be concentrated around the Malay dagger (keris), which was the personal weapon of the aristocrat and the cannon, which was to be found only in the stockades of chiefs.[10]

---

[1] Sultan Abdul Samad of Selangor was said to hold much of his wealth in tin ingots (Gullick (1953), p. 93) and some of it in brass cannon (Middlebrook (1951), p. 90).

[2] Journal of J. W. W. Birch enclosed with PCE.

[3] Swettenham (1948), p. 135.   [4] See above, pp. 96 and 109.

[5] See above, pp. 107 and 109.

[6] Wilkinson and Winstedt (1934), p. 140 for tax collection. The insignia borne by the herald in the Ikat diri episode described at p. 120 above included weapons.

[7] Winstedt (1947), p. 41 and see above p. 67.

[8] PCE.   [9] Skeat (1900), pp. 325–32.

[10] The literature on dagger and cannon is extensive—much of it in JMBRAS, As examples see especially G. C. Woolley (1947), pp. 60–104; A. E. Coope (1947).

Another matter to be considered is the relation of military prowess to the achievement of political power. As has been explained military initiative depended on the provision of munitions. It could thus happen that political leaders did not do their own fighting and that famous captains could be left in helpless inactivity for lack of resources. There still remains the question—was prowess in war an avenue to success in politics? Did the successful fighting man mature into a powerful chief? On the whole the political prospects of a good fighting man of aristocratic birth were poor. It was a matter of temperament and character. A successful captain (*panglima*) was a daring leader of raiding parties. In action he showed murderous courage. Off duty he tended to be quick-tempered and impulsive, much feared as a personal enemy but not steady enough to be a useful ally in politics and government. It thus happened that the most famous bravoes of the period were political failures.[1] On the other hand the successful political leaders had not usually been notable fighters.

Prowess in war was an avenue to prestige and as such a safety valve for a ruling class which by its values tended to breed turbulent young men. The successful fighting man attained to the circle around the men who held power but he rarely became one of them.

[1] As examples Raja Yusuf of Perak in his younger days (see above, pp. 11–12), Raja Mahmud and Raja Mahdi of Selangor and Yam Tuan Antah of Negri Sembilan, who was described by various European observers as 'proud', 'truculent', and 'flighty'. There is a character study of Raja Mahmud in Swettenham (1948), p. 191: 'he feared God but had no sort of fear of man'.

pp. 126–9, followed by F. W. Douglas (1947), pp. 117–18. One interesting aspect of cannon magic is that most of the fixed cannon (but not the light swivel guns) to which these beliefs related were of European manufacture; see Gibson-Hill (1953), p. 143.

7

Economic Aspects of Political Leadership

Political power in the Malay States rested on the control of manpower. In order to attain and hold power a chief had to have a sufficient following of armed men at his back. He must therefore command the means to support a sufficient following. Revenues for this purpose could be obtained from taxing a prosperous, and therefore populous, district. The chief aimed to promote the development of his district and to increase its productive population so as to maximize the surplus which could be diverted into his own hands as the instrument of power.

If he failed to make his district reasonably prosperous he risked being ousted by an outside rival since he lacked the means to support an adequate force with which to maintain his military position. Alternatively the chieftainship might be lost to his lineage (most probably to his own son) at his death and given to someone who would make better use of the opportunity. So long as he retained his district he must be alert to see that no one else accumulated resources sufficient to support a revolt.

The colloquial and idiomatic Malay expression for 'helpless' is *tiada daya upaya*—to be without stratagem and resources. The importance of skill and guile was always recognized.[1] The significance of material resources (*upaya*) is obvious enough but its use in this terse compound phrase is notable.

From what has been said it follows that a chief's interest in diverting the economic surplus of his district into his own hands was to channel essential resources into his control and out again rather than to retain them for personal consumption or accumulation of capital. His privileged position consisted not in exceptional consumption of goods but in exceptional control of services, i.e. the services of his household, his armed following and intermittently of his peasant labour force. To command those services he had to be able to feed those who rendered them. There was an inflow of goods and money to the chief in the exercise of the political function of taxation and an outflow in the requital of services essential to the maintenance of his political position.

This situation gave rise to a problem. The chief had to distribute the wealth which came into his hands. Only by sharing his income with his followers could he hold them to him. The political value placed on the

[1] Wilkinson (1907) stresses this point in the opening passage of his essay on *Malay Proverbs on Character*.

maintenance of a large following was a perpetual inducement to augment the number of his dependents up to the limit of what he could afford. Any surplus which he could accumulate was laid out in loans to bind to him yet more debt-bondsmen.[1] Loans to debtors however were not recoverable at short notice. Sale of bondsmen to other creditors took time to arrange and no doubt involved some loss of prestige (just as their acquisition had augmented it). A chief, even if relatively wealthy, had little surplus income in liquid form available for other purposes such as opening a new tin-mine, agricultural development, etc. The few chiefs who held part of their wealth in 'quick assets' had an exceptional freedom of manoeuvre.[2]

As a preliminary to discussing the economic position of the chief in more detail, something must be said of the Malay economic system generally.

By far the greater part of the surplus of production over producers' consumption needs which could be drawn off as 'political funds' came from tin-mining. By 1870 tin-mining was mainly in the hands of Chinese. It has already been explained[3] that the degree of control exercised by Malay chiefs over Chinese mining communities varied with the size of those communities. In the very large mining centres, such as Larut and Kuala Lumpur, the miners were independent and paid taxes to Malays only if the latter stood between them and the coast ports from which they exported their tin. The more common case was a mining community which managed its own affairs but paid royalty to the landowner on tin produced, export duty on the tin exported and also import and excise duties on spirits, gambling booths, etc. Where the Chinese labour force was very small the Malay chief might even be a partner sharing in the profits of the mine. But whatever the relation between Malay chief and Chinese taxpayer, the revenue from mines was generally the mainstay of the chief.

Malay chiefs also obtained revenue by taxing their Malay subjects. Except in the Krian area of Perak there was no taxation of the main crop, padi. Taxes were imposed on almost all varieties of trade goods. The Malay peasant economy was by no means self-sufficient. Rice was imported in some deficiency areas; salt, dried fish, opium, oil, coconuts and textiles were all staple trade commodities which could be taxed (usually at a 10 per cent *ad valorem* rate paid in kind) as they passed the chief's riverside stockade. There was a small export trade in hides, rattans, gutta percha and other forest produce. Local foodstuffs were sold to Chinese miners. But the Malay balance of payments was apparently preserved only because of substantial 'invisible exports' in the form of money paid by Chinese miners to Malay chiefs and redistributed by the chiefs to their followers.

It was quite usual for Malay aristocrats on a journey to take goods with them for trade. By courtesy one chief did not tax the goods in transit of

[1] See above, pp. 99–105.   [2] See above, pp. 108 and 122.   [3] See above, p. 24.

another.[1] Aristocrats were thus at an advantage in competing with other traders. But they traded only intermittently and on a small scale as journeys undertaken for other reasons afforded an opportunity of doing so. There was however a notable exception in the group of Indonesian traders of quasi-aristocratic status who made a business of business.[2]

The collection of taxes, whether on the tin produced by Chinese miners or on the trade goods destined for Malay and Chinese consumers alike, was correlated with the distribution of political power. In theory the Sultan and other holders of royal offices, such as the Raja Muda, were entitled to collect certain taxes throughout the State. But it was not feasible for them to maintain tax collectors in every district who could neither be supervised nor supported at a distance from the capital. It was inevitable that each district chief should collect all the taxes paid in his district. He was supposed to remit to the Sultan the proceeds of the royal dues. In practice it appears that the Sultan rarely received all that was due to him from outlying districts. He was forced to rely on what he could collect at the royal capital which typically lay at the mouth of the main river-highway into the State.

The inability of the Sultans to obtain more than a small proportion of the total revenues of the State, especially of the taxes on tin which became so important during the nineteenth century, was the main factor which caused a dispersal of power from the central government of the State to the districts. In 1870 this dispersal of power had been an accomplished fact for at least a generation past. The holders of ministerial offices in the Sultan's government had scattered to become district chiefs in order to obtain their share of the revenues.

British administrators who took over the collection of taxes from Malay chiefs in 1874 accumulated a mass of information, though somewhat fragmentary, on the yields of these taxes. From this data the following generalizations can be hazarded. The Sultan who still obtained the import duties levied at the mouth of the main river of the State and also the chief of an important mining district had annual incomes of $25,000 to $100,000 or more.[3] Between these wealthy potentates and the general

[1] In 1875 the Laxamana of Perak was indignant with the British Resident whose customs post had stopped and searched the boat in which the Laxamana was travelling. The gist of the complaint was that it was a breach of a customary immunity. Nonetheless Malay chiefs did sometimes levy taxes on each other's cargoes. Swettenham (1951), p. 53 mentions that Raja Yusuf of Senggang on the Perak River taxed some goods of the Laxamana.

[2] These were mainly Bugis from the Celebes. They often bore the prefix *Nakhoda* (captain of a trading vessel). In Perak in the 1870's the most prominent of this group was Nakhoda Terang. He was a Bugis who, among other interests, was a partner with a Chinese in the firm to which the Sultan had let the tax farms. He became the third husband of Che Mida, widow of the brother of the all-powerful Mentri of Larut. His sister was a secondary wife of the Sultan.

[3] Sultan Abdullah of Perak let the right to collect taxes at the mouth of the Perak River for $24,000 p.a. The lessees, who had to bear the cost of collection,

run of aristocrats there was a wide gap in income. For example in the 1880's an annual income of $6,000 was considered great affluence compared with aristocratic incomes of ten years before.[1]

There is a further index of aristocratic incomes in the allowances granted to Malay chiefs by British administrators when they took over tax collection in 1874. It was said that the allowance granted to each chief was 'at least as large as the income he had hitherto enjoyed'.[2] These allowances were in most cases not less than $600 p.a. and ranged up to $2,400 p.a.

It must of course be taken into account that aristocrats had other minor sources of income besides their tax revenues. They had the profits of trading and tin-mining on a small scale. The food which was consumed by their households was produced by the agricultural workers among their debt-bondsmen.[3]

Against cash incomes of up to $200 p.m. ($2,400 p.a.) must be set the heavy cost of maintaining an adequate following of armed men and domestics. A follower cost about $4 p.m. to support but part of this expense would be met in kind by food supplied by debt-bondsmen. Nonetheless the maintenance of the ten to thirty followers, which was the minimum requirement for the prestige of being a chief or man of position, was a heavy drain on the resources of an aristocrat.

The position of a Sultan was even worse in that he above all others was expected to keep open house for the poor.

'The people look to their chiefs and especially the Sultans for assistance whenever they are in difficulty and they expect to receive it.'[4]

Apart from household expenses a chief had to provide clothing for himself and his womenfolk and also (to a limited extent) for his followers. The finery of Malay aristocrats and their women must have been relatively

---

[1] *SSD*, 14 September 1886—a reference to the situation in the Kinta district of Perak compared with what it had been a few years before.

[2] Swettenham (1948), p. 225. It can hardly have been true of the very wealthy chiefs.

[3] See above, p. 102.

[4] *SSD*, 24 September 1890. In 1889 the Sultan of Pahang estimated his household expenditure at $2,000 p.m. (*SSD*, 5 August 1889). The Sultan of Perak's figure was $4,000 p.m.; he said he had 60–100 people dependent on him and he would abdicate if his allowance was not increased to $4,000 p.m. (*SSD*, 15 August 1889 and 24 September 1890).

---

obtained about $30,000. *PCE*. The revenues of the Sultan of Pahang from import duties levied at the mouth of the Pahang River amounted to $50,000 p.a. (*SSD*, 1 October, 1887). The Mentri of Larut at his peak (1870–2) obtained $180,000 p.a. from the mines of Larut. Raja Juma'at of Lukut, in the early 1860's, had an income of $120,000 p.a. (*SSD*, 13 August 1878).

expensive.[1] A chief had also to provide his women with jewellery.[2] Sultan Yusuf of Perak, a miser, hoarded jewellery to the value of $50,000 in addition to articles given to his womenfolk—but this was an exceptional case.[3]

Much of this expenditure on followers, clothes and jewellery can be related to the twin objects of power and prestige. So too, the chief's house, the largest item of his expenditure on consumers' capital goods. The significance of the layout and structure of a chief's house has been mentioned.[4] Malay custom did not call for the provision of furniture; mats and hangings were all that were usual. But in the 1870's there was just beginning an inclination to furnish in the European style. Thus it is recorded that Che Mida, an aristocratic lady of Kuala Kangsar in Perak, was particularly proud of her bed.[5] Sultan Abdullah of Perak had a table and chairs in his reception room.[6] Syed Hamid, chief of Tampin in Negri Sembilan, had bronze hanging lamps, wall lamps, framed pictures, a ship's clock, a large Turkey carpet and several small carpets in his house.[7]

Such resources as a chief could spare for economic development were usually employed in financing tin-mining, which offered the prospect of the largest and most rapid returns. For example the Dato' Shahbandar of Sungei Ujong in Negri Sembilan had a part share in some twenty Chinese mines; his average stake in each mine was $1,000.[8] Tunku Ahmad Tunggal of Kuala Pilah in Negri Sembilan also had about $20,000 invested in small mines.[9] Between 1840 and 1860 Malay chiefs had laid out very large sums in financing mining development in the Klang valley of Selangor.[10]

It was very often not their own money however which they risked on these ventures. The financiers, European and Chinese, of the Straits Settlements were apparently reluctant to supply food and stores on

[1] There are descriptions of Malay costume in Swettenham (1948), p. 191—Raja Mahmud of Selangor—and Swettenham (1895), p. 163—Raja Yusuf of Perak.

[2] There are some interesting incidental data on Malay purchases of jewellery in the list of the looted stock-in-trade of a Chinese jeweller at Pekan, the royal capital of Pahang, in 1888. Of his stock worth $4,000 in all, very few articles were priced above $100; some only $3. *SSD*, 3 July 1888.

[3] *SSD*, 20 August 1887.   [4] See above, pp. 109–11.

[5] Swettenham (1951), p. 31 and McNair (1878), p. 169.

[6] *PCE*—evidence of Syed Mashhor—'There was a long table; I sat at one end, the Dato' Sagor at another. This was in the Sultan's balai. . . . There were three other chiefs sitting on chairs beside the Dato', and one beside me'.

[7] Syed Hamid had the misfortune to suffer a raid by his neighbour, the Undang of Rembau, in which all this property was stolen. He made a complaint to the British authorities (*SSD*, 28 February 1883). Living within twenty miles of Malacca he was more exposed to European cultural influence than most chiefs.

[8] *SSD*, 29 December 1874.   [9] *SSD*, 20 April 1876.

[10] Gullick (1953a), pp. 87 and 89.

credit direct to the Chinese headman of a small mine. He might default or cheat them. Still more he might be robbed by the local Malay chief. They therefore preferred to go into partnership with the chief so that he would have an interest in supervising the mine and ensuring that it was allowed to succeed. They supplied the miners' requirements to the chief and he passed them on to the miners. So much did they come to rely on this system that it was said of the Dato' Shahbandar (see above) that he was the mainstay of mining in his district.

Apart from promoting mining in their districts it was expected of a chief that he would do what he could to encourage the development of peasant agriculture. The direct loans of a chief to his debt-bondsmen were in some cases a productive investment. The more usual mechanism of promoting new settlement and production was more complex. The usual arrangement was that an Indonesian immigrant, a commoner but a man of some standing and repute, would obtain the chief's permission and help in a project to establish a new village. The founder of the village, as its first headman, advanced money or food to tide new settlers over the first three or four lean years while their fields were worked up into full cultivation and fertility. Aid of this kind was essential. A British District Officer wrote:

> 'It is hopeless to introduce foreigners into the country unless the Government are prepared to offer them work for at least six months in the year during the first three or four years after their arrival.'[1]

In the period before the British regime it was the recognized practice for the chiefs to provide the capital with which a village headman financed his new settlers:

> '. . . provided the Government would advance money, *as the native Rajas had done*, to enable them to open mines and gardens.'[2]

Among particular cases there was the Dato' Dagang of Selangor (a Javanese of quasi-aristocratic status) who took up 600 acres of land around Klang in 1884 and developed it as a coffee estate using Javanese settlers.[3] Commercial monocultural ventures of this kind were however unusual. Another instance was Dyang Ismail, a Bugis merchant in Perak, who said:

> 'I have also introduced about 100 Bugis into Perak, and I have supported them during all the disturbances.'[4]

[1] *AR*, District Officer Kuala Langat, 1891 (*Selangor Gazette*, 1892). It is still the practice to make 'colonization grants' spread over three years to settlers in new padi areas.

[2] Hugh Low in a report on debt-slavery dated 14 December 1878. He was discussing the reactions of Malay aristocrats to his suggestion that they should settle their debt-bondsmen on the land. It was particularly expected of a Sultan that he would provide money for agricultural settlement. (*SSD*, 10 November 1888).

[3] *AR Sel*, 1894.   [4] *PCE*.

It is perhaps significant that most of the known instances are Indonesian merchant adventurers. It is uncertain to what extent the chiefs of long-settled families provided money for peasant settlement. Tin-mining was the favourite investment of this kind.

A few chiefs built short distances of bullock-cart tracks to open up their districts—especially for mining. The Mentri of Larut who made a few miles of road at Larut is mentioned as almost unique.[1]

It has been stated[2] that for various reasons Malay peasants did not build any but the simplest and most temporary irrigation works. The construction of such works on a larger scale was often the best means of opening up an area for settlement. Occasionally a chief promoted such works at his own expense. The Mentri of Larut is said to have built the first irrigation canal at Krian in Perak. The most famous instance is the twenty mile canal from Kedah Peak to Alor Star in Kedah which was built by Wan Mat Saman in the 1880's.[3]

The economic activities of Malay chiefs may be viewed as a particular illustration of a general proposition. Power tends to absorb into itself the control of all spheres from which a rival power might grow. It is in its nature totalitarian. Malay chiefs controlled the economy of their districts because they needed the surplus above the producers' needs to sustain themselves and the armed following which was the basis of their power. Moreover they feared to allow anyone else to become rich and thereby have the potentiality of setting up a rivalry in power.

Wealth being merely a means to an end was used to that end, i.e. for political rather than economic purposes. Most of the money which came into the hands of a Malay chief was used for an immediate political purpose, the maximization of his military power and prestige. It was the obvious and dominant purpose in his mind. To 'plough back' part of this income in order ultimately to augment his resources still further was too remote and indirect a plan to hold his attention. The money which he did invest in development was often borrowed in such circumstances that it could not be diverted to a political end.[4]

There is nothing unusual in this situation. The potlatch of British Columbia, the broad but undeveloped acres of the English landed gentry of a century ago are examples of how political values can distort the use of economic resources and run counter to purely economic considerations.[5]

[1] Swettenham (1948), p. 118.   [2] See above, pp. 28–9.

[3] AR Kedah, 1909.   [4] See above, p. 130.

[5] Cf. Nadel (1951), p. 139: 'One institution may develop as it were by its own momentum in such a manner that it interferes with the efficient working of others, even though it may bear on them in some regulative sense.'

8

The Cohesion of the State

The account which has been given of the Malay political system serves to illustrate the overlap in function of social institutions. Few institutions serve a single purpose only; few social needs are met completely by the functioning of a single institution. Thus political institutions serve mainly to preserve order within a society—but they also have secondary functions of a different kind. On the other hand order is preserved in part by other institutions besides the political system.

For the purposes of this paper the Malay political system has been sufficiently considered in its relation to the spheres of law, defence and economic activity. To sum up that aspect, there was an extension of political authority into these wider fields. In essentials however there was no difference of role in political leadership thus extended. As judge, war-leader, tax collector and provider of funds the Malay chief was exercising a political authority in order to preserve the basis of that authority. If there had been an independent judiciary, a national or popular army, or a non-aristocratic class of capitalists, the whole balance of political power would have been altered. By exercising a multi-purpose authority in so many fields of activity the Malay chief prevented the emergence of any alternative focus of power in competition with himself.

Political institutions operative in non-political fields is one half of the situation. The other was the existence of factors predominantly non-political yet contributing to the effectiveness of the political system. If this idea be spread to its widest possible limits, it becomes absurd. A political system is a means of enforcing order and control. As such it presupposes the existence of a society subject to order and control. The political system is part of and related to the general structure of its society. The whole social structure being mutually adapted to the political system can be said to contribute to the effectiveness of that system.

It is however in a narrower and more specific sense that this theme is propounded here. A political system both requires as a pre-condition of its own existence and by its functioning serves to create a cohesion or solidarity of the community. As an extreme example it is impossible to apply political control to a purely random collection of people, such as a crowd gathered to look on at the result of a street accident. The purely temporary aggregation of people united in a passing interest lacks the necessary cohesion. A policeman can bid the crowd to 'move along, please', but no one can govern it. A musical society or a football supporters' club has sufficient permanance but is based on too narrow a range of common activity (as compared with the totality of social interests) to serve as the basis of political control. A political system must be built upon the general cohesion and 'in group' aggregation of its society. It demands loyalty to its symbols as well as fear of its authority.

In the context of the Malay States the obvious bases of human aggregation were residence, communications and participation in a single economic system. The village was the convenient unit of common residence.[1] The peasant economy of the villages was by no means autarkic and dictated a system of communications and participation in an economic system, both based on the use of rivers as the main channels of movement and trade.[2] As a result there had to be a measure of peaceful intercommunication and trade over the area of a river basin. It was impossible for people to live in inland villages unless traders serving their needs could (at a price) pass the villages nearer the sea. These factors determined the extent and frontiers of the Malay State.

If these factors had been all, one would expect to have found a relatively strong and centralized system of government in each State. But the Malay techniques of communication and political organization were incapable of operating as a unitary system of control over so large an area. Within the State power was dispersed among district chiefs.

There was thus a conflict or balance of centrifugal and centripetal forces. The 'King's Peace' over the area of a State was an economic necessity. On the other hand the instinct of the chiefs in the exercise of their power was to break up the State into smaller warring districts. To a considerable extent the Malay States did break up into anarchy and civil war with results in terms of economic chaos and depopulation which have been mentioned.[3] But there was never a total disintegration and no chief ever sought to set himself up as an independent ruler.[4] The object of every civil war was to secure control of the united State as the power behind the Sultan. The remainder of this section is a review of the factors of integration in this situation.

There were two classes in each State—the rulers and the subjects—and the situation in each class must be separately considered. The ruling class was comparatively homogeneous. It was a closed caste recruited by descent from former members. Only exceptionally were outsiders admitted and then only if they appeared to be aristocrats like the rest.[5] The ruling class

---

[1] See above, p. 29. [2] See above, p. 27.

[3] See above, p. 29.

[4] The Mentri of Larut in Perak was suspected by the British of aspiring to establish himself as an independent ruler but this view was based on a misunderstanding of his pretensions (Wilkinson and Winstedt (1934), p. 98). Larut, unlike most districts, had its own communications with the sea.

[5] See above, pp. 79–81.

was accustomed to cement political connexions and alliances by inter-marriage.[1] The ties resulting from these unions were of considerable importance:

> 'Amongst the higher classes everyone knows everyone else, and relationships are recognized even to what seems remote kinship.'[2]

This situation did not prevent intrigue and feud between rivals who were sometimes close kinsmen. It does seem however to have facilitated reconciliations when the struggle had gone far enough. It prevented a complete and permanent split in the ruling class.

The ruling class thus inter-related by descent and marriage shared common values and traditions. Above all else it esteemed political status expressed in titles, written genealogies (*salasilah*), personal retinues, the shape of houses and other outward and material demonstrations of distinction. Status of course depended on the reality of power. A lineage which failed to provide the holder of a traditional office went under. The important point is however that it was not enough to be powerful. The fruits of office included the title and insignia conferred by the Sultan and acknowledged by the aristocratic circle of the State. These things were valued for their own sake and not merely as incidental appurtenances of power.

The significance of the outward dignities of power contributed to the preservation of the Sultanate, however impotent the Sultan himself might be. The Sultan was the fount of nobility and therefore the essential apex of the prestige system. Aristocrats fighting for the reality of power sought the formal approval of the Sultan for their cause.[3] Their whole code of status was shaped in the pattern of the Malacca Sultanate, the heroic age of the Malay States. They had broken up the central government of the Malacca city state,[4] but they had preserved its titles of office for their use as district chiefs. The charter of these titles was conferment by the Sultan. Without such a charter, and the consequent recognition of their peers, the titles were of little value.

Any form of status is essentially a social or relative phenomenon. It consists in the recognition by the members of a group of the special position of one or more of their number. In the Malay States the need for recognition of high status was a factor in strengthening the unity of the State against the inherent weaknesses of the dispersal of power. Status derived from conferment of titles by the Sultan; without that there could be no claim to recognition. But it was not enough to hold a title by indisputably legitimate charter from the Sultan. There was also need of a system in which status might be demonstrated and recognition demanded. It was for example an empty dignity to be one of the four chiefs of the first rank unless this superior status could now and then be demonstrated by

[1] See above, pp. 83–9.

[2] Swettenham (1900), p. 142.

[3] See above, p. 49.

[4] See above, p. 11.

participation in the ceremonial around the Sultan in which all the chiefs were present each in his appointed place. The humility of abasement[1] before the Sultan was also a source of pride in that the chiefs came forward, one by one, in descending order of seniority to abase themselves. The chiefs were thus driven by their own need of acknowledged status to preserve the Sultanate and to maintain a degree of peace and order in the State to permit occasional gatherings at the royal court.

The absorption of the Malay ruling class in the achievement of prestige was reflected in an elaboration of cultural media concerned with the expression of prestige. It was an example of the familiar phenomenon of a social preoccupation, pattern or focus of interest in one element of the culture of the society.[2]

Among the subject class the situation was quite different. Cultural homogeneity usually stopped at the limits of the village, i.e. two neighbouring villages were often self-consciously different in their cultural pattern. There were villages of men who had immigrated, or whose forbears had done so, from Menangkabau, Siak, Batu Bahara, Acheh, the Batak district and other parts of Sumatra. There were Bugis from the Celebes, men of Java, Banjarese from Borneo and more besides. They shared a common Indonesian substratum of cultural essentials. But they were at least as conscious of their differences as of their similarities.[3]

Nonetheless it is remarkable that in each State there was a sense of national (i.e. State) solidarity. The Perak Malays, said Swettenham, had 'an exceeding dislike for and jealousy of all foreigners (including Malays not of Perak)'.[4] The Negri Sembilan Malays too distinguished themselves from others by their tradition:

> 'We, sons of Menangkabau, who dwell with the heavens above us and the earth beneath our feet, who once held the lands round the Mighty Burning Mountain as far as the great pass that opens the way to the plains, who migrated down to Silagundi, to the territories below the State of Sumatra in the isle of Andalas.'[5]

The notable fact about this myth of origin was that it was shared not only by descendants of immigrants from Sumatra in Negri Sembilan but also by the *waris* clans descended from headmen of the Malacca Sultans[6] and by immigrants from Acheh, Java and elsewhere who had become absorbed into the Negri Sembilan polity. They had united around a dominant cultural theme and they treated it as the national heritage of them all.

[1] See above, p. 48.

[2] E.g. Herskovits (1948), p. 542: 'Cultural focus designates the tendency of every culture to exhibit greater complexity, greater variation in the institutions of some of its aspects than others'.

[3] See above, pp. 25–6.   [4] *AR Pk*, 1890.

[5] Wilkinson (1908b), p. 8 where the Malay text is cited.

[6] See above, pp. 25 and 39.

This situation is at first sight rather surprising. There was not only cultural heterogeneity within the subject class of each State. There was also cultural homogeneity stretching across State boundaries. For example Perak as well as Negri Sembilan had a considerable element of Menangkabau immigrants among its population.[1] Yet the Malays of Perak and the Malays of Negri Sembilan regarded each other as foreigners.

There was no sense (or at least no expression) of a Malay world including all the States of the Peninsula, Sumatra, Borneo and elsewhere united by ties of migration and trade. The individual Malay State, although a mere part of the Malay world, was the largest unit which was conceived as a unit. There is even a Negri Sembilan saying in which the word for 'world' is used to denote 'State'.[2]

At this point there is a danger of the argument chasing its own tail. It is suggested as an hypothesis that the subject class of each Malay State was united in a sense of belonging together as a group and that this sense of social cohesion supported the State as a political unit. Yet it has to be admitted that the subject class of the State had little consciousness of anything in common except in terms of belonging to the State as a political unit.

The difficulty is resolved however by distinguishing between the political system in its primary function as a means of control and the political system in its secondary function as part of the common cultural heritage of the society. Its secondary function can create conditions favourable to the performance of the primary function. It is here submitted that this was the position in the Malay States.

It seems inevitable that a government must always create a sympathy or an antipathy, a loyalty or an urge to revolt, among the governed. Submission to external, social control is to some extent unwelcome to any individual however gregarious. The half-suppressed resentment at being controlled must find its outlet in aggression either in support of the regime or against it.

In the most usual case the government is valued as part of the national tradition. As an example consider the British attitude to their own variety of parliamentary democracy. It can happen however, as it did in some parts of the Austro-Hungarian Empire, that a clash develops between the popular sense of a national culture and the prevailing political system

---

[1] See above, p. 25.

[2] *Raja menobat didalam alam;*
Penghulu menobat didalam luhak.
The king rules his world;
The chief rules his province.   Wilkinson (1908b), p. 24.

Also quoted more briefly as *Alam beraja, luak berpenghulu; Alam* is a word of Arabic origin which is generally used to denote the world or universe. Its usage to mean a kingdom is peculiar to the Menangkabau/Negri Sembilan culture. Wilkinson (1932).

which is hated as alien. Such a conflict may arise over an issue not inherently political.[1] But it goes to establish the proposition that a community feels the need of having a government which it can regard as compatible with its own national tradition or culture. This attitude is one of the mainsprings of colonial nationalism.

The need to have political institutions which can be identified with the nation is particularly strong among populations of mixed cultural origin. It was so in the Germano-Slav Bohemian provinces of the Austro-Hungarian Empire. It appears in the vehemence of American sentiment about the American constitution and the 'American way of life' (a distinctly political concept). In such cases cultural diversity of origin has given rise to a strong sense of solidarity centred round the political system as a symbol. Where cultural differences create lines of fission owing to infrequent 'interaction'[2] the weakness is remedied by exceptional significance attributed to what is common to all. It is suggested that among the subject class of the Malay States a somewhat similar situation existed.

The subject class in the Malay States were certainly not united by the same interests as the ruling class. They had no interest—in terms of enhanced status—in the dignities of office and the ceremonies of the Sultan's court. There were no public ceremonies at which any considerable number of the subject class gathered and shared in a common sense of unity. The poor communications and scattered population of the Malay States made it impossible to convene such gatherings. There was however a general popular awareness of the Sultanate as the apex of the system. This feeling was expressed in the belief that the Sultan could influence the prosperity and welfare of the State for good or ill.

The most important element of political cohesion of the subject class was their relationship with the members of the ruling class who were their particular masters. It was this relationship which they had in common. It was an attitude blended of loyalty and a cynical awareness of their own helplessness in face of oppression.

The sense of loyalty to the chief was noted by observers as follows:

'The spirit of the clan is also strong within him. He acknowledges the necessity of carrying out, even blindly, the orders of his hereditary chief, while he will protect his own relatives at all costs and make their quarrel his own.'[3]

'The position of the people to their chiefs is that formerly occupied by a clan in Scotland to its chief. They will do his bidding and take harsh treatment from him more contentedly than from anyone else.'[4]

It is notable that two observers independently[5] hit on the comparison

[1] One of the major sources of conflict between the Malayan Chinese and the present regime is policy on and control of Chinese education.

[2] Homans (1951), e.g. at pp. 35–7.   [3] Swettenham (1895), p. 4.

[4] Clifford, *SSD*, 15 October 1887.

[5] They were not entirely 'independent' though there is no reason to think that there was any conscious borrowing of ideas. Clifford on first arrival in Malaya in

K

with the 'clan' as they conceived it and defined the attitude of the Malay peasant to his chief in terms of quasi-kinship ('clan'—'hereditary chief'). In this respect the attitude of the peasants to their chief differed from the symbolic and magical role attributed to the Sultan. The latter was not 'the father of his people'.

The relations of peasants and chiefs became the subject of a proliferation of proverbs. This group of proverbs, taken with the related proverbs on class distinctions,[1] indicate the preoccupation of the peasant class with this aspect of their social relations. The proverbs are a cynical, bitter code. The arrival of a chief and his followers in a village is likened to the very destructive incursion of a wild elephant.[2] Resistance to authority is as futile as a goat fighting a tiger.[3] The small man may get a few pickings at the table of the great,[4] but he runs the risk of perishing in the ruin of his patron like ticks on a dead fowl.[5] He should avoid becoming involved in the quarrels of the great, like a mousedeer crushed between fighting elephants.[6] In the last resort it is better to run amuck than to perish by inches; rather be eaten by a crocodile than nibbled by small fish.[7] It is not suggested that Jack is as good as his master; lack of manners will always betray lack of birth.[8]

The political wisdom of Negri Sembilan was a rather happier variation on the theme of the importance of knowing one's place and of following the proper procedure. Pound rice in a mortar, boil rice in a cooking pot.[9]

It was the wisdom of a common code of conduct. They all had to be wise in this fashion in dealing with their chiefs, to bear the same ill-treatment and oppression or to avoid it by the same stratagems.

ISLAM AND MAGIC

The sharing of a common political situation was not the only bond of sympathy which bound together immigrants and sons of immigrants from so many different parts of Indonesia. They were all (with the unimportant exception of the Batak) Muslims. They had been converted to

[1] See above, p. 65.
[2] *Gajah masok kampong.* Brown (1951), p. 94.
[3] *Bagai kambing dengan harimau.* Op. cit. p. 95.
[4] *Besar kayu besar bahan-nya,* Big logs make big chips. Op. cit. p. 95.
[5] *Mati ayam, mati tungau-nya.* Op. cit. p. 97.
[6] *Gajah sama gajah berjuang, pelandok mati di-tengah.* Op. cit., p. 97.
[7] *Biar di-telan buaya, jangan di-pagut ikan kechil.* Op. cit. p. 98.
[8] *Usul menunjokkan asal.* Op. cit. p. 59.
[9] *Menumbok di-lesong, menanak di-periok.* Wilkinson (1908b), p. 17.

1884 was sent to be trained in the office of the British Resident of Perak, a post in which Swettenham was then acting. They served as administrators in the Malay States—though never again in the same State—until after the passages quoted above had been written.

Islam for some five centuries. It was however a conversion which permitted the retention of much of the Hindu ritual which had been practised in the pre-Islamic period together with a still older stratum of Indonesian paganism. The result of this mixing of creeds was rich and various. It was by no means uniform in texture but it constituted a common amalgam by which the Malays of all classes were united rather than divided.

Islam was not to any significant extent a 'state religion'. There was no priesthood other than the vicars of village mosques (*imam*) who were of the community and did not form a caste apart, and the chaplains of the more devout Sultans and chiefs who never attained any collective importance in the political system owing to lack of organization. There were no major public rituals of Islamic content. At the installation and funeral of a Sultan there were indeed Islamic prayers and elements in the ritual but these did not make the proceedings essentially Islamic. The most important purely Islamic occasions were the annual feast-days[1] at which it was customary for a Sultan or chief to hold a levee at which his subjects presented their respects.

There were no *Kathis* (Muslim judges and registrars) until the era of British protection.[2] Islamic legal doctrine appears in the Malay legal codes but there is no evidence to show that this doctrine, or any part of the codes, was effective law.[3]

There are of course instances of individuals who were pious Muslims. Some prominent figures lived their lives according to the faith. Sultan Ismail of Perak, for example, refused except in the most urgent cases to transact business by affixing his state seal to a paper on a Friday (the Muslim day of prayer).[4] Sultan Idris of Perak, after a rather dissolute youth, became devout in early middle age. Before his installation as Sultan in 1887 he spent several days in fasting and prayer; he had a chaplain who was a Muslim divine.[5] But personal piety of this kind, unsupported by a priesthood or by public ceremonial, does not make a State religion.

Islamic learning was an avenue to prestige, though rather at village level than among the aristocracy. A Muslim divine (*Sheikh*) of Arab descent or a returned pilgrim to Mecca (*Haji*) was always entitled to respect.

[1] The celebration of the end of the month of fasting (*Ramadan*) called *Hari Raya Puasa* in Malay; the climax of the pilgrimage to Mecca (*Hari Raya Haji*); and the Islamic New Year (*Maulud*). See also n. 1 at p. 47 above.

[2] Perak had its first Chief Kathi in 1880 and Selangor in 1885; neither was a member of the old ruling class.

[3] See above, p. 114.

[4] This appears incidentally in a remark by a witness before *PCE* that the Sultan sealed a paper on a Friday, which he had never been known to do before.

[5] The fasting and prayers are reported in *SSD*, 15 April 1889. Swettenham (1895), p. 208 mentions that he asked the Sultan for information of *berhantu* (seance) practices. The chaplain drew him aside afterwards and reproved him for mentioning such matters.

Descent from the Prophet Mohamed (marked by the honorific prefix 'Syed') carried many an Arab half-caste into high society to which he might otherwise have had difficulty in attaining.[1]

Islamic prestige and Indonesian magic sometimes became associated in the same person. In the 1890's Ungku Sayid, a celebrated divine and magician of Kuala Trengganu, played some part in the Pahang War.[2] There was a holy man at Rekoh in Selangor whose tomb became a shrine after his death.[3]

The two institutions of Islam which assumed some political importance were the system of religious instruction and the pilgrimage to Mecca. There was no lay education in the Malay States at this time. At most a chief found a wandering schoolmaster from the Straits Settlements (British territory) as tutor for his sons. It was customary however for boys of all classes to be instructed at about the age of puberty in reading the Koran and in the tenets of Islam. In most cases they went to learn from the leading divine of their village. He would be a pilgrim to Mecca who had perhaps lingered on in Arabia to improve his knowledge or who had in his time been the pupil of some more famous teacher. The boys were taught to read the Koran in Arabic parrot-fashion and they seldom progressed to a real mastery of Arabic or a profound learning of Islamic doctrine. Ability to read the Koran well was a source of social prestige. It was associated with the attainment by an adolescent of adult status.[4]

There were also famous religious teachers who took pupils from a distance to live with them during the period of instruction.[5]

The pilgrimage to Mecca served two different purposes according to the class of the pilgrim. For the villager it was an opportunity to gain

---

[1] See above, p. 67.

[2] *AR Phg*, 1894. It was feared that he would rouse the Pahang Malays into a sort of holy war against the European infidel. In the event he attracted little support—in Clifford's opinion the Pahang Malays were too lax in their faith to launch a *jehad*.

[3] *Selangor Gazette*, 1894.

[4] Swettenham, held up at Pangkor (Perak) in 1874, noted in his diary, 'I have taken to reading the Koran with the Penghulu; there's one comfort in it that I understand it as well as anyone else here, and that is not at all. There are only about six Malays in the Straits who do understand it tho' at least half of them can read it.' Swettenham (1952), p. 37. He was at this time a rather supercilious young man though a brilliant scholar of Malay.

The circumcision of boys at puberty followed the period of instruction in the Koran. At a Malay wedding the bride was privately catechized by a party of divines to find out if she knew a phrase or two of the Koran—as a sign of fitness for matrimony.

[5] A District Officer in Pahang in 1905 reported an 'annual exodus of the youth of the district to Patani and Kedah to seek that religious instruction which is not apparently to be found to any extent in Pahang'. *AR Phg*, 1905. The improvement in communications and security may well have increased this traffic over the past twenty years.

status. The returned pilgrim for the rest of his life bore the title *Haji* before his name preceded by the honorific prefix *Tuan* (Sir). The pilgrimage was an expense beyond the resources of the ordinary villager.[1] It was an opportunity open to a headman or to a member of a leading or wealthy village family. In a list of thirty village notables and headmen at Rembau (Negri Sembilan) in 1883 there are six who were *Hajis*.[2] It is unlikely that twenty per cent of the entire village populations had made the pilgrimage. For the vicar of a mosque (*imam*) it was a usual though not obligatory qualification to have made the pilgrimage.

For the aristocrat the pilgrimage afforded an opportunity of withdrawing from a social environment in which he had lost face. After an interval he then returned with sufficient prestige to offset any remnants of his previous embarrassment. Swettenham comments:

> 'The pilgrimage to Mecca is the cure for the errors of the Mohammedan world. The lady whose liaison has become public property; the man who has seduced his sister-in-law; or, like Wan Hamid, been too heavy-handed in beating his enemy; these perform the pilgrimage, and return with repaired reputations and an odour of sanctity that enables them to resume their places in society without loss of caste.'[3]

The field of magic, like that of Islam, does not require a lengthy survey in the context of the political system. Sultans were believed to have magical powers but these were the passive consequence of being invested with the royal office rather than the result of activity as a magician.[4] Magic, like Islam, was not a 'state religion'. The nearest approach to such a situation was when the Sultan fell ill. The magical rituals which were performed to promote the recovery of any sick man were then performed on a scale appropriate to the dignity and importance of the sick ruler. There was a seance at which the medium was an aristocrat.[5] The ceremonial was elaborate. Wilkinson relates how the court magicians, who were close relatives of the Sultan, performed rites on a nine-tier stage erected for the purpose. The rite included an invocation of 'the Spirits of the Country . . . in the strict order of their precedence. . . .'

> 'A strange assembly was this ghostly Court of Perak. It numbered among its aristocrats spirits borrowed from all religions and from every part of the world, souls of orthodox rulers like Ali, Ahmad and Solomon, deities of India

[1] *AR NS*, 1892 records a remark by Yam Tuan Mohamed of Negri Sembilan to the effect that the main inducement for the accumulation of cash by a Malay peasant was the hope of eventually making the pilgrimage. A pilgrim who died at Mecca enjoyed special prestige in this world and the next. It was an inducement to make the pilgrimage in old age and thus spend the savings of a lifetime.

[2] *SSD*, 23 February 1883.

[3] Swettenham (1900), p. 161.

[4] See above, pp. 44–6, especially p. 46.

[5] Swettenham (1895), p. 4 in his account of the illness of Sultan Yusuf of Perak says of the medium: 'In ordinary life she was an amusing lady named Raja Ngah, a scion of the ruling house on the female side and a member of a family skilled in all matters appertaining to occultism'.

like Brahma and Vishnu, nature gods like the Supporter of the Heavens and the Ruler of the Storm and divinities of special localities like the Dato' of Mount Berembun.'[1]

On the first day the protective deities were invoked; on the second day their help was sought; on the third the Sultan, if cured, was ritually bathed.

A ceremony of this kind was magic for the welfare of the State embodied in the Sultan. There is a more debatable question in the construction to be placed on a seance (*main berhantu*) conducted by Sultan Abdullah of Perak in 1875. Abdullah driven to exasperation by the first British Resident of Perak, held a seance, at which he himself was a medium, to enquire of the spirits how Perak might be rid of the troublesome Mr. Birch. In this case there can be no question but that the Sultan was invoking the Spirits of the State not so much for his own personal welfare as for the removal of a threat to the State. But was this episode typical? Abdullah himself was a man of unstable temperament and some personal eccentricity. The other Malay aristocrats are reported to have laughed when Abdullah first suggested holding a seance for this purpose. One of them refused to attend it because he regarded it as incompatible with the tenets of Islam. Another of them described the ceremony afterwards in a rather contemptuous tone and said that he had never before witnessed such a performance.[2]

It is probable that such acts of public magic under the direction of the leaders of the State occurred only in times of grave national crisis such as the illness of a Sultan, the spread of epidemic disease or possibly the threat of external attack.

Organized village magic was commonly practised under the leadership of the village headman in order to drive out pestilential spirits which might injure health or crops. The most common forms were a mock battle in which the victors, representing the village, drove out another party which represented the evil ones.[3] In another form the evils of the village were put out into midstream of the river in a model boat to float away to the sea.[4] The rituals of rice cultivation occurred at every stage in the seasonal cycle from first clearing of the ground to harvest.[5]

The village magician was usually a member of the community. If local practitioners had failed to produce satisfactory results he might be a

[1] Wilkinson (1908a), pp. 37–8.

[2] These facts were elicited in evidence before the commission which enquired into the murder of Birch. The best account of the seance by a witness is quoted by Wilkinson and Winstedt (1934), pp. 172–4.

[3] The writer has known a ceremony different in detail but similar in purpose used by Malay chiefs to repel smallpox in Negri Sembilan in the troubled times of 1945.

[4] Skeat (1900), pp. 433–6; Winstedt (1947), p. 16.

[5] Skeat (1900) and Winstedt (1947).

distinguished expert invited from outside. In either case he worked in alliance with the headman. Apart from public ceremonies the magician also practised magic for the cure of illness and the solution of personal problems such as the recovery of lost property.

There is a distinction to be made between participation in public rituals and the mere sharing of a common corpus of belief. There were only infrequent occasions for ceremonies, whether pagan or Islamic, to draw together the people of the State. There was no organized priesthood or order of magicians. On the other hand the sense of being all Muslims together played its part in uniting people otherwise divided by many cultural differences. It is significant that to be a Muslim was equated with being a Malay.[1] It implied membership of a society as well as of a church. The willingness to try an outside practitioner when the local magician failed was a recognition of a common body of pagan ritual and belief. It was limited to the Malays; their magic did not operate among outsiders.[2]

To sum up, the heterogeneous villages of the Malay States were held together in a larger community by something more than the fear of their chief and of the men at his back. They were conscious of themselves as people of a State whose welfare depended on the good or bad genius of their Sultan. They shared a common relation of subjection to their chief. They were bound to him by ties of loyalty and yet were sagely cynical about the risks and misfortunes which came to them at his hands. In the worship of their God and in the magical procedures for obtaining supernatural help and blessing they were aware of what they shared. On this foundation of partial social cohesion the political system was built.

[1] The expression for conversion to Islam is *masok Melayu*—to enter into the Malay.

[2] Skeat (1900), p. 41 relates an incident which shows that a Chinese was considered to be immune from the supernatural penalties to which a Malay was susceptible if he touched the royal regalia.

Appendix Sources

The published works consulted in writing this study are listed in the next section, References and Abbreviations.

The other information comes from official records. During the early years of British intervention in the Malay States a long series of despatches were written by Governors of the Straits Settlements to the Colonial Office. The despatches themselves are not usually of great interest. But they are supported by reports and memoranda written by administrators with present or past experience of the Malay States. Some of the most interesting of these papers are the reports on the political history and situation of Perak, Selangor and Negri Sembilan written in 1874 by Thomas Braddell, Attorney General of the Straits Settlements; the reports on Malay 'debt-slavery' written by various administrators in 1875 and again in 1882–3; the report of the commission of enquiry into the causes of the Perak War of 1875; and the memoranda of 1883 on Malay village headmen. But there is an immense amount more to be gleaned here and there from less promising papers.

In the early years senior administrators reported to their superiors by keeping official diaries which were sent in periodically. From the early 1880's the diaries were replaced by annual reports. These papers are of decreasing interest as the years after 1874 go by, but the earlier ones are valuable sources.

The value of these working government papers is that they are contemporary records whereas the published memoirs of prominent administrators are conscious efforts at literary composition written twenty years or more after the event. None of the administrators in question was a conscious ethnographer and on some subjects, such as 'debt-slavery' or the inefficiency of Malay methods of administration, they were biassed in their observation. But the best of them were first-rate Malay scholars with a scientific interest and an aesthetic appreciation of Malay culture as a whole.

The more important of these official writers of reports were:

(1) *Thomas Braddell* came to the Straits Settlements in the 1840's as a planter. He was later a police officer and then Attorney General. He played a leading part in the negotiations which brought Perak and Selangor under British protection in 1874. He retired about 1881. His knowledge of Malay personalities and dynastic questions was encyclopedic. In his later years he was one of the recognized panel of experts on Malay affairs who advised the Governor in Singapore. The other three members of the panel were Irving, McNair and Swettenham.

(2) *Hugh Clifford* came to Malaya in 1883 at the age of seventeen as a cadet in the civil service. He served mainly in Pahang between 1887 and 1900. After a long period away from Malaya he returned as Governor of the Straits Settlements in 1927. A superb scholar of Malay and author of several books on Malay life.

(3) *Hugh Low* served for nearly thirty years in North Borneo before coming to Perak in 1877 as British Resident. He retired in 1889. He is famous for his brilliant success in developing a modern system of administration in the Malay States. His success was in part due to his understanding of the Malay point of view.

(4) *William Maxwell* began his administrative career in the Straits Settlements in 1869. He was Assistant Resident of Perak at Larut in the late 1870's and early 1880's and British Resident of Selangor from 1889 to 1892. He was the author of numerous articles on Malay custom in the Journal of the Straits Branch, Royal Asiatic Society.

(5) *Fred McNair* first came to the Straits Settlements as an engineer in the Indian Army. After retiring from the Army he became Colonial Engineer (Director of Public Works) in the Straits Settlements in 1868. He took a great interest in Malay affairs and was employed on various political missions in 1874-5. He retired in 1883. Author of a book called *Perak and the Malays* published in 1878.

(6) *Frank Swettenham* is quoted more in this study than all other sources put together. He came to the Straits Settlements as an administrative cadet in 1870. He was employed on political missions in Perak and Selangor in 1874-6. Later he was British Resident of Selangor and then of Perak; first Resident General of the Federated Malay States; and finally Governor of the Straits Settlements. Author of several books on the Malay States and Malay life and a brilliant scholar of Malay. He died only in 1948.

Abbreviations and References

I. ABBREVIATIONS

Journals

JMBRAS	*Journal of the Malayan Branch, Royal Asiatic Society*, 1923–55 (Continuation of *JSBRAS*).
JSBRAS	*Journal of the Straits Branch, Royal Asiatic Society*, 1880–1922.
MHJ	*Malayan Historical Journal*, 1954–.
PMS	*Papers on Malay Subjects* (Published in Kuala Lumpur by the F.M.S. Government Printer).

Official Papers

AR	*Annual Report* (followed by the year to which it refers).
NS	Negri Sembilan.
Phg	Pahang.
Pk	Perak.
Sel	Selangor.
PCE	Report and Evidence taken by a Commission of Enquiry into the events leading to the Perak War of 1875. Sent to London under cover of *SSD*, 14 December 1876. Public Records Office volumes CO 273/6–8.
PSC	*Minutes of Perak State Council.* PMS 1907 and 1909.
SSD	Despatch (including memoranda enclosed with it) from the Governor of the Straits Settlements to the Secretary of State for the Colonies (followed by the date of the despatch). Public Records Office series CO 273 and CO 809.

II. REFERENCES

ABDULLAH MUNSHI (1955).	The Hikayat Abdullah, an annotated translation by A. H. Hill, *JMBRAS*, xxviii, Pt. 3.
BROWN, C. C. (1951).	*Malay Sayings.* London.
(1952).	*The Malay Annals* (translation), *JMBRAS*, xxv, Pts. 2 and 3.
COOPE, A. E. (1947).	The Floating Cannon of Butterworth, *JMBRAS*, xx, Pt. 1.
DOBBY, E. H. G. (1950).	*Southeast Asia.* London.
DOUGLAS, F. W. (1947).	The Penang Cannon Sri Rambai, *JMBRAS*, xx, Pt. 1.
EVANS-PRITCHARD, E. E. (1940).	*The Nuer.* Oxford.
FIRTH, R. W. (1929).	*Primitive Economics of the New Zealand Maori.* London.
FORTES, M. and EVANS-PRITCHARD, E. E. eds. (1940).	*African Political Systems.* London.
GIBSON-HILL, C. A. (1953).	Dutch Cannon found in Malaya, *JMBRAS*, xxvi, Pt. 1.

GULLICK, J. M. (1949). Sungei Ujong, *JMBRAS*, xxii, Pt. 2.
(1953a). A careless, heathen philosopher? *JMBRAS*, xxvi, Pt. 1.
(1953b). Captain Speedy of Larut, *JMBRAS*, xxvi, Pt. 3.
(1954). The War with Yam Tuan Antah, *JMBRAS*, xxvii, Pt. 1.
HERSKOVITS, M. (1948). *Man and his Works*. New York.
HOMANS, G. C. (1951). *The Human Group*. London.
INNES, E. (1885). *The Chersonese with the Gilding Off*. London.
JONG, P. E. DE JOSSELIN DE (1951). *Minangkabau and Negri Sembilan*. Leiden.
LINEHAN, W. (1936). History of Pahang, *JMBRAS*, xiv, Pt. 2.
(1951.) Traces of a Bronze Age Culture, etc., *JMBRAS*, xxiv, Pt. 3.
MAHMUD BIN MAT (1954). The passing of slavery in East Pahang, *MHJ*, Pt. 1.
MALINOWSKI, B. (1922). *Argonauts of the Western Pacific*. London.
MAXWELL, W. E. (1890). Malay Debt Slavery, *JSBRAS*, x.
McNAIR, J. F. (1878). *Perak and the Malays*. London.
MIDDLEBROOK, S. M. (1951). Yap Ah Loy, *JMBRAS*, xxiv, Pt. 2.
NADEL, S. F. (1951). *The Foundations of Social Anthropology*. London.
PANNIKAR, K. M. (1953). *Asia and Western Dominance*. London.
PURCELL, V. (1948). *The Chinese in Malaya*. London.
RADCLIFFE-BROWN, A. R. (1952). *Structure and Function in Primitive Society*. London.
RIGBY, J. (1908). The Ninety-nine laws of Perak (translation), *PMS*.
SKEAT, W. W. (1900). *Malay Magic*. London.
SWETTENHAM, F. A. (1880). Independent Native States of the Malay Peninsula, *JSBRAS*, i.
(1895). *Malay Sketches*. London.
(1900). *The Real Malay*. London.
(1948). *British Malaya*. London.
(1951). Perak Journals, 1874–6, *JMBRAS*, xxiv, Pt. 4.
TWEEDIE, M. W. F. (1953). The Stone Age in Malaya, *JMBRAS*, xxvi, Pt. 2.
VLIELAND, C. A. (1932). *A Report of the 1931 Census of Malaya*. Singapore.
WALES, H. G. QUARITCH (1940). Archaeological Researches on ancient Indian colonization in Malaya, *JMBRAS*, xviii, Pt. 1.
(1947). Further work on Indian sites in Malaya, *JMBRAS*, xx, Pt. 1.
WILKINSON, R. J. (1907). *Malay Proverbs on Character*. PMS.
(1908a). *Incidents of Malay Life*. PMS.
(1908b). *Malay Law—an Introductory Sketch*. PMS.
(1911). *Notes on the Negri Sembilan*. PMS.
(1924). *Events Prior to the British Ascendency and Notes on Perak*. PMS.
(1932). *Malay-English Dictionary*. Smyrna, 1902. Rev. edn, 1932.
WILKINSON, R. J. and WINSTEDT, R. O. (1934). History of Perak, *JMBRAS*, xii, Pt. 1.

WILSON, G. (1951).   The Nyakusa of Tanganyika, *in* Colson, E. and Gluckman, M., eds, *Seven Tribes of British Central Africa*. Manchester.

WINSTEDT, R. O. (1932).   History of Johore, *JMBRAS*, x, Pt. 3.

(1934a).   History of Selangor, *JMBRAS*, xii, Pt. 3.

(1934b).   History of Negri Sembilan, *JMBRAS*, xii, Pt. 3.

(1935).   Malaya and its History, *JMBRAS*, xiii, Pt. 1.

(1939).   History of Malay Literature, *JMBRAS*, xvii, Pt. 3.

(1947a).   *The Malays. A Cultural History*. Singapore. Revised edn, London, 1950.

(1947b).   Kingship and enthronement in Malaya, *JMBRAS*, xx, Pt. 1.

(1950).   *Malay Proverbs*. London.

WOOLLEY, G. C. (1947).   The Malay Keris, its origin and development, *JMBRAS*, xx, Pt. 2.

Index

LONDON SCHOOL OF ECONOMICS
MONOGRAPHS ON SOCIAL ANTHROPOLOGY

Titles marked with an asterisk are now out of print. Those marked with a dagger have been reprinted in paperback editions and are only available in this form.

*1, 2. Raymond Firth, *The Work of the Gods in Tikopia*, 2 vols, 1940.

*3. E. R. Leach, *Social and Economic Organization of the Rowanduz Kurds*, 1940.

*4. E. E. Evans-Pritchard, *The Political System of the Anuak of the Anglo-Egyptian Sudan*, 1940.

5. Daryll Forde, *Marriage and the Family among the Yakö in South-Eastern Nigeria*, 1941. (Available only from International African Institute)

*6. M. M. Green, *Land Tenure of an Ibo Village in South-Eastern Nigeria*, 1941.

*7. Rosemary Firth, *Housekeeping among Malay Peasants*, 1943. (Revised edition in preparation)

*8. A. M. Ammar, *A Demographic Study of an Egyptian Province (Sharquiya)*, 1943.

*9. I. Schapera, *Tribal Legislation among the Tswana of the Bechuanaland Protectorate*, 1943. (Revised edition in preparation)

*10. W. H. Beckett, *Akokoaso: A Survey of a Gold Coast Village*, 1944.

11. I. Schapera, *The Ethnic Composition of Tswana Tribes*, 1952.

*12. Ju-K'ang T'ien, *The Chinese of Sarawak: A Study of Social Structure*, 1953.

*13. Gutorm Gjessing, *Changing Lapps*, 1954.

14. Alan J. A. Elliott, *Chinese Spirit-Medium Cults in Singapore*, 1955.

*15. Raymond Firth, *Two Studies of Kinship in London*, 1956.

16. Lucy Mair, *Studies in Applied Anthropology*, 1957.

†17. J. M. Gullick, *Indigenous Political Systems of Western Malaya*, 1958.

†18. Maurice Freedman, *Lineage Organization in Southeastern China*, 1958.

†19. Fredrik Barth, *Political Leadership among Swat Pathans*, 1959.

20. L. H. Palmier, *Social Status and Power in Java*, 1960.

†21. Judith Djamour, *Malay Kinship and Marriage in Singapore*, 1959.

22. E. R. Leach, *Rethinking Anthropology*, 1961.

23. S. M. Salim, *Marsh Dwellers of the Euphrates Delta*, 1962.

24. S. van der Sprenkel, *Legal Institutions in Manchu China*, 1962.

25. Chandra Jayawardena, *Conflict and Solidarity in a Guianese Plantation*, 1963.

26. H. Ian Hogbin, *Kinship and Marriage in a New Guinea Village*, 1963.

27. Joan Metge, *A New Maori Migration: Rural and Urban Relations in Northern New Zealand*, 1964.

28. Raymond Firth, *Essays on Social Organization and Values*, 1964.

29. M. G. Swift, *Malay Peasant Society in Jelebu*, 1965.

30. J. F. Boissevain, *Saints and Fireworks: Religion and Politics in Rural Malta*, 1965.